http://www.fa

Church ...dens
Reflections on 1600 years of Management,
Ministry and Maintenance

Author – Eric Sanderson

Copyright © Eric Sanderson (2019)

All rights reserved.

No part of this publication may be reproduced, stored in a retrieval system, or transmitted in any form or by any means, electronic, mechanical, photocopying, recording or otherwise, without the prior permission in writing from both the copyright owner and publisher of the book.

Front cover illustration: Hexham Abbey
(a painting by Arthur Blackburn) Copyright © 2019
Cover design by Author.

ISBN 978-178456-622-7

First published 2019 by FASTPRINT PUBLISHING
Peterborough, England

I have tried to ensure accuracy, however should you find any errors or omissions please let me know.
eric.sanderson3@virginmedia.com

About the Author

Eric Sanderson was born in Newcastle upon Tyne in 1946. The family engineering business roused Eric's curiosity in all things mechanical. His education at Atkinson Road Technical School and later at John Marlay Secondary School led him to an apprenticeship with GPO Post Office Telephones. After many years as a telephone engineer he became a Business Systems Quality and Compliance Auditor with British Telecom. Eric retired from BT in 1999, but to stop work – never! He shares the view of Ian Bruce, the Scottish folk songwriter, who in 1995 described retirement in his song 'Blue Denim Days' – bright and breezy, free and easy! Retirement allowed Eric more time to indulge in his pastimes of walking, writing general interest articles for his church magazine, family history and building sets for his local theatre. He served as churchwarden at St Peter's Monkseaton in the Newcastle diocese, and now lives in Cheshire with his wife Elaine and their faithful Border Terrier dog called Zac.

ACKNOWLEDGEMENTS

I would like to thank my wife for her patience whenever I disappeared into the study for hours on end. At first, she may have wondered why it was taking so long to write the book, but having now read it, she appreciates Oscar Wilde's view on patience.

History books always struck me as boring , so I am grateful for permission to use the work of three astute observers of church life: Ron Wood , Noel Ford and Dennis Fletcher , three worthy cartoonists who are regular contributors to the Christian press. Their cartoons are so apposite . If you are not familiar with their work, please look them up, you won't be disappointed.

My thanks go to Helen Myers for assisting with initial editing and proofreading ; also to Sam and her designers at Printondemand -worldwide for their patience in managing what was a steep learning curve for me. Any errors that remain are entirely my own.

Posthumous thanks go to family antecedents who led interesting (and at times colourful) lives, which have helped me to inject a personal perspective into the narrative of this book.

The cover picture is one of the many watercolour paintings created by my father -in-law , Arthur Blackburn. He was untrained and always considered himself an architectural draughtsman, rather than an artist . Nevertheless the naivety of style in his paintings give them a charm of their own.

Foreword

The ancient ecclesiastical office of churchwarden is an intriguing one. Despite many ups and downs, this office, the highest of lay positions in the Anglican Church, has stood the test of time.

The office of churchwarden was the first of the parochial institutions to be politically contested, which led to the formation of civic corporations and Parochial Church Councils. I have not dismissed this fact, but have avoided discussion as it has been well documented by worthy academics and is a subject in its own right.

Having had the privilege to serve as churchwarden, I was curious to find out about the life and times of those who performed the role in the past. What I found was that the challenges facing churchwardens today pale into insignificance when compared to the wardens of yesteryear.

There have been many books written to assist churchwardens in discharging their duties, detailing their responsibilities with respect to the intricacies of ecclesiastical law. Some made the role seem quite a challenge. What I hope to bring you is lay persons view of the churchwarden through the ages; from the early years of the Christian Church to the present time. By examining the important roles they have played in parish life, along with the challenges they faced whilst interpreting complex laws and social problems throughout the ages, will perhaps reassure current post-holders that they are indeed better off than their predecessors.

When studying history at school I became disillusioned by the focus on royal genealogy and insistence on memorising dates, when what I really wanted was to know *how* people lived. To paraphrase a popular Monty Python question: 'What did the churchwardens ever do for us?'

INTRODUCTION

In 1841, Charles Grevile Prideaux QC (Balliol College, Oxford and bencher of Lincoln's Inn) chose the following words for the dedication of his book:

A Practical Guide to the Duties of Churchwardens in the Execution of their Office.

'To all who may enter upon the office of Churchwarden with an earnest desire conscientiously to discharge their important functions, and, by upholding the fabrics of the Church, by preserving due reverence within the Consecrated Precincts, and by checking to the utmost all gross impiety and immorality in their parishes, to promote the glory of God and the well-being of their fellow-parishioners, this book is respectfully dedicated.'[1]

Sadly, I am not gifted with the same eloquence as Mr. Prideaux in providing such a forthright dedication for this book. All I can say is that I hope you enjoy this time-traveller's guide to the role of churchwarden.

As the Archdeacon of Canterbury succinctly put in the foreword to the *Churchwarden's Yearbook 2016*:

'As new vicars come and go, the churchwardens bear witness to a tradition which has sustained the Church over past decades.'[2]

ALTERNATIVES TO 'CHURCHWARDEN':

Fabric warden (pre-1500s)
Church reeve (from 1386)
Kirkmaster (from 1429)
Churchwarden or chapelwarden (from 1466)

Contents

Chapter 1	In the Beginning	15
Chapter 2	The Office of Churchwarden	27
Chapter 3	Records	38
Chapter 4	Preachers	48
Chapter 5	Control of the Congregation	52
Chapter 6	The Churchwardens Staves	61
Chapter 7	Misdemeanours	63
Chapter 8	Involvement of the Churchwardens in Civil Duties	71
Chapter 9	Financial Management	82
Chapter 10	Settlement and the Poor Law	86
Chapter 11	Beating the Bounds	92
Chapter 12	Social Fundraisers	96
Chapter 13	Religious Dissention & Recusancy	107
Chapter 14	The Rise of Non-Conformance	110

Chapter 15	Presentments and Visitations	113
Chapter 16	Environmental Management	122
Chapter 17	Witchcraft and Magic	125
Chapter 18	Peculiers	128
Chapter 19	The Election of Churchwardens and PCC	130
Chapter 20	Checks and Balances	136
Chapter 21	The Public Worship Regulation Act	140
Chapter 22	The Organ Snatchers	143
Chapter 23	Flares and Graces (and Bling)	145
Chapter 24	Notable Churchwardens	150
Chapter 25	Churchwardens Today	162
Chapter 26	The Times They Are A-Changin'	167
Chapter 27	Entrepreneurs and Impresarios	172
Chapter 28	Tempus Neminem Manet	174
Chapter 29	The Future	177

Chapter 30	Has the church gone barking mad?	181
Chapter 31	In Praise of Churchwardens	184
Bibliography		186-195
Additional Reading		196
Credits		197
Epilogue		199

Chapter 1

IN THE BEGINNING

When researching the origins of the churchwarden, I became aware that the first references to the role in religious places of worship appeared before the birth of Christ, when *gabbaim* (or *shamashim* – men of all work) were active in the Jewish synagogues. These laymen, chosen by the people, were unpaid members of the synagogue whose role was to ensure the smooth running of services and collection of charitable donations for distribution to the poor. Later, in Acts 6: 1-4, Luke relates that certain apostles were concerned that widows were being overlooked in the daily distribution of food. It was suggested that seven of their number should be nominated to carry out lay ministry tasks, allowing the remainder to devote their time to prayer ministry. Later in the Bible, in 1 Peter 4: 10, we hear Peter declare, 'Each of you should use whatever gift you have received to serve others, as faithful stewards of God's grace in its various forms.'

The first reference to the office of a Christian churchwarden appears around 1600 years ago, in an ecclesiastical history of the fourth century, when St Augustine refers to certain church officers as *Seniores Ecclesiastici*. These officers had care of the utensils, treasures, etc., and correspond to modern churchwardens or trustees. They may be considered to be the ecclesiastical ancestors of our present churchwardens.

By the 11th century, the bishops decided that they needed reliable people who could report to them on the conduct of clergy and their congregations. However, there are few (if any) direct references to churchwardens and their responsibilities prior to the 12th century. It was not until diocesan statutes were issued by Bishop Peter Quinel in 1287[3], requiring the annual presentation of written accounts, that we start to see accounts of churchwardens appear. Initially, the detail recorded was vague and inconsistent, limited by the literacy and numeracy of the clerks, although some parishes (if their finances allowed it) might have employed scribes to assist.

The office of churchwarden is one of the oldest recognised forms of lay ministry and is the highest position of trust and responsibility that the Church gives to its lay people. Their appointment was required by an edict of the Council of London in 1127 (Synod),[4] and later in the Rolls of Parliament of 1341 they were described as 'wardens of the goods of the church'. They also appear in parish records from around the 13th century. By the mid-15th century, they were elected by parishioners and undertook responsibility for the church fabric, and by the mid-17th century, they had acquired a very high profile in 'parish management'.

Churchwardens have survived through frequent changes of faith, alternating between Catholic and Protestant as monarchies changed. They have protected churches and their possessions from feudal barons, grappling with monarchs and megalomaniacs to maintain democracy. Over the centuries, churchwardens became men of many 'hats', acquiring tasks that required a broad range of both practical and pastoral skills. Powers and responsibilities varied from parish to parish, making some churchwardens influential, whilst others were less so.

I have teased out interesting and fascinating pieces of information from many sources, ranging from timely accounts, historical writings and newspaper cuttings, attempting to illustrate the churchwarden's role. I have highlighted the responsibilities, relationships, trials and tribulations which would have made the role both fulfilling and challenging, as they attempted to manage the difficult trichotomy of taxman, policeman-cum-spy and welfare worker, all whilst being a member of the parish community they served. I have tried to give a balanced view, however, as they say – 'bad news often makes better copy than good news'.

Churchwardens are 'special', devoted people; able to donate time, energy and sometimes money to the parish whilst having the ability to concurrently support themselves, their businesses and family. A good example of this was my wife's fifth great-grandfather, who in the mid-18th century served as both churchwarden and overseer whilst running a quarry business supplying stone to the great houses of Gloucestershire. He was also a listed sculptor, yet he still found time to father fifteen children by two wives! Perhaps we should add 'stamina' to that list of qualities.

Very few people were exempt from nomination and in medieval times, to virtually anyone – except 'non-conformists' (Jews and Catholics, but not Quakers) – even illiteracy and innumeracy was no bar. Should a non-conformist have been nominated for the role, they would have chosen to appoint a deputy in their stead in order to maintain their principles. If the preferred churchwardens were illiterate, then a paid scribe would have been provided, or the parish clerk appointed to help with keeping records. Side-stepping the role, however, would have incurred payment of a fine. The following groups were exempted service *if they personally objected*: peers, sheriffs, clergymen, members of the House of Commons, magistrates, barristers and solicitors, physicians and surgeons, dissenting ministers, officers in the navy or the army on full pay, men in the militia or army reserves, registrars of births, deaths and marriages, and officials of customs, excise, or the post office.[5]

The role of churchwarden was not constant; it was often shaped by social and economic demographics. Local customs and parish legal matters, coupled with manorial or civil government, frequently made the churchwarden's role a political one, mired with mountains of 'red tape'. This required ingenuity, guile and sometimes subterfuge, to juggle crown requirements with matters important to the parish, as well as personal and family responsibilities. The majority of churchwardens were pillars of society; entrepreneurs with a good degree of altruism.

However, we must be reminded that others, along with some Justices of the Peace and vestrymen, might just as easily have been petty despots with their own aims and ambitions to fulfil, rather than sympathetic to the poor and needy of the parishes they served! The good, the bad and the ugly!

Today, the churchwarden is still one of the strangest voluntary occupations imaginable. They are an ecclesiastical jack-of-all-trades, combining intensely practical elements with quietly spiritual or pastoral roles; intermingled with a multitude of legal and financial responsibilities. Unlike their predecessors however, when things get stressful, they can't relax in their personal pew at the back of church and stick their churchwarden's pipe out the window to have a smoke! These pipes, still appreciated by pipe-smoking aficionados, were named after churchwardens (or night watchmen) who, when guarding churches through the night, could not be expected to last the whole night without a smoke. They therefore used pipes with exceptionally long stems so the smoke and the pipe wouldn't be in their line of sight as they kept watch.

N.W.Crute

GOVERNMENT OF THE PEOPLE

Following their victory at the Battle of Hastings, the Normans established a feudal system in England. All land in England was ruthlessly claimed by King William I (the Conqueror) who divided it into 13,418 'manors' (areas of land administration), giving the land and title of 'lord of the manor' to those who were loyal to him. This was not a 'noble' title, but one indicating 'tenant-in-chief'. Reeves were appointed to help with administration.

A reeve was a Saxon term denoting a man with administrative responsibilities; an official position. The Domesday Book suggests that there was a reeve in every habitation and for anything that needed some form of administration, including the church. A church reeve was also known as the *Praetositus Ecclesiae*, or ecclesiastical leader.

Between 1348 and 1350, the Black Death killed nearly half the population, striking a further six times before the end of the century. Labour was in great demand, making it difficult for the lords to impose on serfs and so their powers were diminished. As a result of poor communication (information travelled at the speed of a horse) and weak central government, parish councils began to develop. The parish priest met together with other educated people and villagers to take responsibility for the administration of laws and taxes and to make decisions that affected them (similar to a local government).

ROYAL INFLUENCES

Before the arrival of the Normans, monasteries had long been a feature of the religious landscape. Thirty-five houses of Benedictine monks and nine nunneries appear in the Domesday Survey as possessing land and many of the abbeys were endowed with great estates. This amounted to one third of the farmed land in England. Throughout the following centuries, the monasteries became an increasingly important part of Christianity and the stronghold of the Pope's power in England. Although individual monks avowed poverty, monasteries invariably became very wealthy from donations of land and endowments made by rich people. These people hoped to 'buy' their way into heaven and would be encouraged to purchase 'indulgences' in exchange for absolution at death! The vow of poverty was incongruent with the self-aggrandisement of abbots in rich cloisters, who enjoyed the glittering treasuries and magnificent architecture of the wealthiest monasteries: a striking discord incompatible with the principles of poverty and humility.

In 1085, The Domesday Book records that discipline of the clergy was lax and their morals loose, *however their orthodoxy was beyond reproach.*[6] This would later be confirmed when, in 1535, King Henry VIII appointed Thomas Cromwell to the joint roles of Vicar-General of the English Church and Visitor General of the Monasteries.[7] Thomas's first action was to order a survey to establish the wealth of the monasteries. Later, commissioners (inspectors) visited the monasteries to investigate rumours of idleness, greed and bad behaviour. They reported back advising that the monasteries were indeed 'idle, corrupt and useless' but there was some evidence that religion was 'well-kept and observed'. However, there were also allegations of monks fathering children and getting married. King Henry and Thomas Cromwell, in order to justify their actions, chose to have the more favourable reports re-written to emphasise the laxity of the clergy. This was done to validate the subsequent actions they took to acquire the wealth of the monasteries.

The ruthless dissolution of the monasteries resulted in the loss of works of art and the destruction of valuable pieces of literature. Property was stripped of anything valuable and livestock was seized. In some places where the monastery had been the centre of life, whole communities collapsed and many of those employed by monasteries found themselves without jobs. Some ultimately became vagabonds. The success of Protestant reform depended upon willing collaborators: those with influence. Country gentlemen would enforce Protestant laws by encouraging new ways and beliefs among their servants and tenants. Yeomen and artisans, who might have served as churchwardens, ensured that altars came down, English Bibles were introduced and Tudor coats of arms were displayed. At this point, the last strongholds of Papal power were destroyed and Henry VIII had complete control over the Church in England. The Protestant faith had been violently implemented, although whilst the churchwardens' accounts at the end of Henry VIII's reign acknowledged the ecclesiastical supremacy of the King, few doctrinal changes had been made and the Church remained much the same as it had been.

Henry VIII's daughter Elizabeth I,[8] appreciated that religion had caused many problems for the country's inhabitants so she sought to find a 'middle ground'; one that would be acceptable by both Catholics and Protestants. She believed that people's happiness and the peace of the country came before religious principles. Bibles and church services would be in English and whilst there was still a Catholic flavour in faith and practice, it was sufficiently vague as to allow for a variety of interpretations along the Catholic - Protestant spectrum. Elizabeth firmly believed that people should be allowed to practise the Catholic religion without fear of recrimination provided it presented no threat to peace and her rule over England. The largely illiterate congregation was encouraged to learn to read the Bible and attendance at church was compulsory, at least in theory. Sunday services in the Church of England would have included official homilies, notices and government propaganda – interminable lecturing, followed by a party-political broadcast. [9] Worship was frequently disrupted, as people talked laughed and even slept through services and church-wardens had to employ 'bouncers' to maintain order.

Over the course of around 500 years, Christianity had arrived in England in the form of Roman Catholicism, changed to Protestantism, then back to Roman Catholicism and back again to Protestantism. As churchwardens were parish officials as well as guardians of the faith, regular changes in the monarchy (and hence in religion) may have occasionally caused them consternation. They had to decide whether to 'change sides' to maintain a continuum of parish management expertise and personal status or keep to their religious beliefs and suffer the associated consequences of becoming a recusant (see chapter 13). By the latter part of the 17th century and early years of the 18th century, Anglicanism had an emphasis on simple devotional religion and moral living.

ECCLESIASTICAL ESPIONAGE

It has been said that spying is the world's second oldest profession and the earliest biblical reference is in Genesis 42: 9-11, where Joseph recalls his dream about his brothers and accuses them of being spies. In Biblical scripture, nothing is *explicitly* said about the Wednesday of Holy Week. However, we are aware that from that day, Judas had secretly watched and colluded with the Sanhedrin, waiting for a chance to turn Jesus over to the chief priests. For this reason, many Christians have labelled this day as 'Spy Wednesday'.

Earlier, whilst describing the role of churchwarden, I suggested that it had been created by the bishops to spy on incumbents and parishioners, compelling the churchwardens to manage a difficult trichotomy of policeman-cum-spy, taxman and welfare worker, all whilst remaining a member of the parish community they served. Churches were at the heart of village life and were well attended; all aspects of life were celebrated enthusiastically. During the post-reformation period, this idyllic way of life was shattered when the Machiavellian Thomas Cromwell was appointed by Henry VIII and set about disbanding the monasteries.[10] He was the ideal candidate for the task having previously helped Cardinal Wolsey dissolve monasteries. Thomas had become an enthusiastic promoter of Machiavelli after reading his book, Il Principe (the prince) which suggested that all was acceptable 'if the end justifies the means.' Thomas was a wolf in sheep's clothing who could transform seamlessly from geniality to malevolence as the situation demanded.

There was a fear that the crown would attack the parish churches after the monasteries. It was at this point that the role of churchwarden changed from gamekeeper to poacher, as they vociferously protected their churches from Cromwell's tyrants who began to strip them of their wealth and artefacts. Many parishes secreted or sold property before Cromwell's men arrived, whilst others were less cunning. Their buildings were desecrated and people were left bereft. Churchwardens were minor league when compared to the government spies of the day. Cromwell, though humble by birth, became an expert in law and commerce, mercenary warfare and espionage. He became one of the most ruthless people to dominate English politics, earning himself the epithet 'Prince of Darkness'. Never mind 007, this man was 001! Thomas Cromwell built a network of spies and informers (at home and abroad) and his mastery of the black arts makes the most ruthless of modern politicians seem mild by comparison. He ran a spy network comparable to the KGB, seeing off his enemies on trumped up charges and revelling in torture.[11]

Chapter 2

THE OFFICE OF CHURCHWARDEN

Out of the host of officials appointed by the parish, the churchwardens were the most important. A lay position, it has been legally recognised since its introduction by the first Canon of the Council of Westminster, London, in 1127.[12] There are records of churchwardens being chosen or initially appointed by the bishop or his officers as early as 1200, and by 1500 these records were well established. Churchwardens were elected each Easter Monday and records show that parishioners chose or elected them, giving rise to the notion that the roots of English democracy lie in the medieval parishes. The system of dioceses and parishes developed as a means of keeping a check on the public and preventing the inhabitants of one area from moving to another without the proper permission or authority.

The office of churchwarden evolved to include the role of church treasurer, responsible for holding the parish stock on behalf of the parishioners. To meet these demands on the local community, churchwardens were elected by the parish to look after the church and its ornaments. Later, this would include other secular aspects of parochial administration, such as repairs to, and the upkeep of, roads and bridges. Towards the end of the 15th century, churchwardens gained responsibility for the maintenance of order and decency in the church and churchyard, particularly during the time of divine service. It is not clear how this came about, but as representatives of the parishioners, they tacitly assumed an oversight of the behaviour of those who came to the church, with the dual responsibility of keeping the place in good order and informing the ordinary (the bishop) of those offending against the ecclesiastical laws. They were required to take an oath and make 'presentments' of offenders and report on the state of church buildings, ornaments, furnishings, etc, to the ordinary on his visitation.

In ecclesiastical law (as part of the ancient episcopal synods, which were absolute), 'synodsmen' (sidesmen) or 'questmen' were summoned by the bishops to provide information on the misbehaviour of the clergy and parishioners and to report heretics. As the office of churchwarden evolved, all the duties of the synodsmen were subsumed into the role of the churchwarden who became known as 'the bishop's eyes and ears'. Humphrey Prideaux, the 17th century Archdeacon of Suffolk, described churchwardens as 'ecclesiastical constables'. The post had not been created to assist the incumbent, but to keep an eye on him and his parishioners!

THE VESTRY (PARISH MEETING)

Under the Tudors, parish meetings and their appointed officers were given more and more responsibilities for maintaining the church and they banded together, becoming the smallest unit of local government. Initially, vestry committees were not established by any law, but they evolved independently in each parish according to local needs, from their roots in medieval parochial governance. By the early 17th century, parish meetings were so well organised that they acquired responsibility for all manner of local government and became 'pocket parliaments'.

As the manorial courts began to decline, parish officers became, along with the county magistrates, the rulers of rural England.

The vestry was a meeting of the parish ratepayers that convened when necessary, although with an annual meeting at Easter to audit accounts and to appoint parish officers. They were chaired by the incumbent of the parish and they discussed secular and ecclesiastical business. Originally held in the parish church or its vestry (or sometimes the pub), the meeting became known colloquially as the vestry meeting. They started out as a 'modest reflection over breakfast', consisting of a calf's head (the delicacy of the day), but they later involved a prodigal waste of money being spent on feasting, drinking and gluttony – second of the deadly sins!

Throughout the 18th century, the vestry could take either of two formats: (1) a closed vestry, in which a committee of male householders (typically 24) managed business on behalf of the parish and recruited new members as and when necessary; (2) an open vestry, which included all householders and ratepayers (including women). The annual Easter meeting of the vestry was usually followed by a large celebratory feast, during which all parish officers were appointed to serve for the forthcoming year and the outgoing officers' accounts were audited.

In addition to the churchwardens, officers appointed would include: overseers of the poor, beadles, scavengers, surveyors, collectors and constables. The precise number of officers depended on individual parish requirements.[13]

As senior members of the vestry, the churchwardens (usually two in number) were elected on an annual basis. There was a vicar's warden (chosen by the incumbent) and a people's warden (chosen by the people), although larger parishes could appoint more according to local need. The churchwardens wielded considerable power (greater than the incumbent) and they were the people's representatives in all parochial matters. Their primary responsibilities included setting church and other local tax rates, as well as managing the parish accounts. People brought differing levels of expertise and competence to the role of churchwarden: whilst some were skilled and dedicated, others were less so. They were both guardians of parochial morals and trustees of the church's goods, deriving a good deal of authority from the parish collective. However, groups of householders could be occasionally disruptive, making their task arduous.

ELECTION OF CHURCHWARDENS

In the past, the selection of churchwardens was variable and at times far from democratic, with many idiosyncrasies apparent. There was no right of refusal to serve, however the elected person could opt to nominate a deputy in his stead and pay the requisite fine for doing so. It would appear that this happened frequently, as parish records indicate healthy income in this regard.

Some parishes would choose to rotate the role of churchwarden among householders or they employed a junior/senior warden system, whilst others allowed wives to take over their husband's role after his death. Depending on your perspective, these alternatives might be viewed as prudent succession planning, or at worst, shear nepotism! Female churchwardens were the exception, although there is some early evidence of them being educationally assisted by the guild system, allowing them to participate in family businesses. Wormingford in Essex was significant because it had a near full complement of female parish officers for several years in the late 18th and early 19th centuries. In theory, women could also vote in parliamentary elections prior to 1832, when franchises operated on property ownership and they met the required criteria.

By the late 18th century, autocracy, nepotism and scandal beset the political system, and consequently an Act was introduced to the House of Lords in an attempt to eradicate institutional corruption.

The Great Reform Act of 1832 introduced wide-ranging changes to the electoral system of England and Wales and was designed to correct the many prevailing abuses in the voting system. For the first time, the right to vote was restricted to 'male persons', disenfranchising the many women who had previously voted in town council elections.

The Sturges Bourne reforms of vestry government in 1818 and 1819[14] were introduced to control the spiralling costs of providing poor rate relief resulting from the fallout of the Napoleonic wars and agricultural failures. The reforms redrew a distinction between the 'deserving' and 'undeserving' poor, ultimately changing individuals' and families' entitlement to relief under the old poor laws. The policy-making structure of local government (parishes) was strengthened by the creation of select vestries, consisting of wealthy householders who paid the most parish rates. Excluding the poorer ratepayers was divisive but allowed tighter control when voting on the distribution of poor relief. Whilst the legislation did not specifically exclude women from the electorate, some parishes saw fit to do so as there was no existing local precedent allowing women to vote. In parishes where precedent had already been set, there is evidence to show that women played an active part in local politics.

There are many examples of women performing the roles of churchwarden and overseer, parish clerk and sexton (called a sextoness). Some men were in favour of this and some were against it. In 1835, the

Leeds Intelligencer, one of the first British regional newspapers, expressed the view that all rated women (those paying the parish rate) were entitled to vote as well as men. It explained 'we do not wish for a gynocracy: but we are sufficiently gallant to perceive that too many of the wayward lords of creation are disposed to make a bad world of it: therefore, the sooner the ladies interfere the better'.[15]

Others, however, were not so disposed... The misogynists. In 1684, Mary Jaques was (reluctantly) appointed churchwarden by the incumbent and parishioners of Little Wilne nr. Shardlow in Derbyshire.[16] However, the election was challenged in the courts by Mr Turner (her attorney) who stated that she was not capable of the office and that she should be discharged of her duties as churchwarden. The case was upheld and the parish was ordered to re-run the election. The following year, the court affirmed the 'incapacity' of a woman to serve as churchwarden. It was perhaps citing the precedent set by a learned reader at Gray's Inn, who in 1662 said that although the law did not exclude women from being churchwardens, or overseers of the poor, it was women's incapacity 'for the most part' to learn the law, that rendered them incapable of exercising discretion. A practical reason why women were considered unsuitable for these positions of authority concerned the very real incapacity that they suffered if they married.[17] The debate on the role of women in churches, sometimes referred to as petticoat politicians,[18] continued until the early 20th century, with vociferous debate regarding their position. At that time, the Anglican Church still barred women from most offices and some clergy even refused to allow a woman to take the collection, let alone elect one as a churchwarden (One priest even said that it would be a 'slur on the parish'.)

In some city parishes, there was an assumption that the office of churchwarden was for the local elite and in London, the role was viewed as a status of honour among local communities . As such , it was considered to be a curus honorum[19] - a prerequisite for progression to higher office . Churchwardens were sometimes even addressed as Master or Worshipful.

The churchwarden's duties expanded during the 16th and 17th centuries as more civil responsibilities were assigned to parishes. In the early 18th century, a written manual was produced entitled *The Compleat Parish Officer*, which was no doubt an invaluable handbook for parish officials, helping them to navigate through the plethora of rules , regulations and social problems of the time. This was followed in the early 19th century by *The New and Complete Parish Officer*, ambitiously boasting that it was written in 'easy and familiar terms' and would be useful to parish officers of every denomination ! Today, there are a plethora of self-help books and 'survival guides' to assist churchwardens, but thankfully no-one has stooped so as low as to produce an 'idiot's guide' and Haynes have yet to make an offering!

Today, the only remaining element of the old annual vestry meeting, is the annual election of churchwardens, which takes place before the annual parochial church meeting. (APCM)

The process of swearing in the new churchwardens is enacted annually, at the archdeacon's visitation. This has been the accepted practice certainly since the publication, in 1734, of *The Compleat Parish Officer*. The manual states that neither the elected churchwarden nor the archdeacon have rights of refusal in their elected duties; to do so would invoke a mandamus (writ) being issued by the courts. The churchwarden could be ex-communicated (more than likely a fine would be imposed) and the archdeacon could be reprimanded.

Humphrey Prideaux QC, in his *Directions to Church-Wardens*, states that 'the Archdeacon hath no power to refuse, for the parish have the right of election and are judges of the qualifications of the party by them elected; and if they choose an ignorant or beggarly fellow, it is at their peril, and a Church-warden's office is a temporal office, and a corporation by law, and it cannot be supposed that the Archdeacon should have more care of the parish, than they of themselves, and a peremptory mandamus awarded'.[20]

A Multifaceted Role

At base level, churchwardens had a tripartite role, although there were many sub-levels within it. They were:

(1) Guardians of the parishioners' morals and behaviour.

(2) Temporal Custodians of the church buildings and property (as they still are today).

(3) Guardians of the public parts of the church (nave, porch, belfry and graveyard), but not the chancel which was the incumbent's domain.

As we will see later on, their role involved bringing together a number of elements which made them more akin to the 'chief executive' of the parish. As the bishop's parish representative, they were required, at his request, to attend the archdeacon's visitation. Here, they would report to the bishop on the state of the church's morals, finances and the physical condition of the buildings. The churchwardens would also make 'inquiries' to check that the parson:

- ✓ Read the 39 articles twice a year and the canons once a year.
- ✓ Preached every Sunday, read the common prayer and homilies, and performed the sacraments.
- ✓ Ensured that the parish observed three special days: 30 January (the execution of Charles I), 29 May (the return of Charles II) and 5 November (the discovery of the gunpowder plot).
- ✓ Preached in his gown and wore a surplice.
- ✓ Visited the sick and buried the dead.
- ✓ Catechised and baptised children (with godfathers).
- ✓ Performed marriages according to the law.
- ✓ Lived a sober life.

Chapter 3

RECORDS

The GenGuide (a genealogy aid) tells us that the churchwardens' accounts of old would record comprehensive details of outgoing expenditure relating to all aspects of their responsibility, both civil and ecclesiastical, and would name the individuals to whom the monies were paid. Their reports to the bishop were detailed and personal. Churchwardens would sometimes have to arrange the baptisms of foundlings (abandoned children) and the burials of strangers (see chapter 8 for civil duties).

Churchwardens today are the administrators of the present, custodians of the past and champions of the future. Record-keeping is not the most inspiring part of the churchwarden's responsibilities but probably close to the top of the list of priorities. Records build a history of the church and all the events that have occurred there, which is clearly demonstrated through historic churchwardens accounts.

Records are only useful if they are documented correctly and maintained carefully. The Church of England gives guidance on such matters in a series of documents published by their Records Centre. A good starting point are Records Management Guides No. 1 (Keep or Bin...?) and No. 2 (Save or delete...?).

GLEBE TERRIERS

It may sound like a breed of dog (even the churchwarden's dog), however the term refers to the land and its constituents given as part of a clergyman's benefice, for the time he is incumbent. Glebe terriers were first introduced in 1571 to provide parochial surveys of pieces of land and the tithes they attracted. Churchwardens are still required to keep a detailed terrier and an inventory of all church property. Annually, all these terriers, inventories and logbooks should be produced for the PCC to check and, if necessary, put right any discrepancies and deal with any problems.

The archdeacon can ask to check anything, especially that any property recorded in the terrier is actually present and that any repairs and renovations have been authorised to be carried out. These details, together with all their relevant paperwork, should be kept in a logbook for which the churchwardens are also responsible. They must be prepared to explain, and if necessary to defend, their actions to the archdeacon on his annual 'visitation'.

Even today, the church, churchyard (God's acre) and all movable property is in the temporal custody of the churchwardens. The incumbent has the legal right to use such property for the proper conduct of church services. This means that the churchwardens cannot ban the incumbent from using the pulpit, nor refuse to allow the church silver to be taken out of the safe, so long as the pulpit is the centre of preaching and the silver is used for its proper purpose. By contrast, however, it is perfectly legal for them to exclude the incumbent from the church and to arrest them should the occasion arise! Should a churchwarden resign, they must advise their resignation to the Bishop and pass their keys to their successor.

HAVE YOU GOT A FACULTY?

The PCC is responsible for repairs and maintenance, and the churchwardens own the building's contents (in temporal).

The church, churchyard and parsonage, are not owned by the Church of England, nor by the diocese, nor by the PCC. Our churches belong to everyone. Legally, nobody actually owns England's 16,000 parish churches. They are in the existing 'corporation sole', which is in effect the corporate expression for the 'cure of souls'. With few exceptions, they are held in trust by the incumbent for the parish (not the congregation) to the benefit of not only the worshipping community, but of all parishioners.[21]

Churches can only be used by the parish in accordance with the established rules of the Church of England. There are very strict rules governing the sale or disposal of churches, laid down in Parliamentary Measures. The parishioners can't just vote to sell their church or change it into a bingo hall, nor can the incumbent do anything other than that allowed by the Measure. All churches are subject to planning law, and the Church of England's system of planning control is governed by canon law, ecclesiastical law and heritage law, which forms part of this country's ordinary legislation. Along with the 39 articles and the canons of the Church of England, sits the faculty jurisdiction, the Church of England's regulation of works on church buildings, their contents and churchyards. It exists to ensure that all work is planned and managed sympathetically. The faculty jurisdiction of the Church of England goes back to medieval times.

Works to all Church of England buildings (whether listed or not) have been controlled for many centuries by the Consistory Courts of the Church. Under the provisions of the Care of Churches and Ecclesiastical Jurisdiction Measure 1991, all works, alterations and additions to parish churches, their churchyards and contents require faculty approval. It is the duty of the minister and churchwardens to obtain a faculty before carrying out any alterations (subject to *de-minimis* lists provided by each diocese). It is unsurprising that there are few instances of unauthorised works to churches, given the Christian conscience. However, mistakes do happen, arising from ignorance or impatience due to the intricacies and slow pace of the system, rather than the pig-headedness of the incumbent or PCC.

However, deliberately flouting the authorities is not unknown and the results can be catastrophic.

For example, a PCC once sold fine silverware without any authority, a vicar once covered the floor of his chancel with ceramic tiles, thinking (wrongly) he had a faculty, and some churchwardens once sold medieval furniture for much less than their true worth. In many cases, there is no desire to reverse any works completed, as they are acceptable to all. In such cases, a confirmatory faculty (not retrospective) may be appropriate: where there has been genuine ignorance on the part of the petitioner about the need to obtain a faculty. Such a faculty legitimises future work but not previous actions, which remain illegal for all time, and for which disciplinary proceedings and criminal prosecutions may ensue, under both civil and criminal law.

Faculty *Faux-Pas* - The following examples should serve as a salutary lesson to all churchwardens and those applying for a faculty. They demonstrate the importance of knowing the rules and good record-keeping. Beware: ignorance may be bliss but it is no defence in law.

A grave matter - In 2011, the rector and churchwardens (plus some others, collectively referred to as 'the building party') had applied for a faculty for permission to build a school building within the grounds of the Grade I listed Christ Church Spitalfields in London. [22]

The faculty was granted and unopposed by the diocesan chancellor. However, it was later challenged by a local action group on the grounds that it contravened the Disused Burial Grounds Act 1884, which makes it unlawful to erect any public building on a disused burial ground, except for the purpose of enlarging the church or another place of worship. Describing the offence as cultural and environmental vandalism, the appellant sought to overturn the faculty and have a restoration order applied, which would return the site to its previous state. The church was very lucky not to be prosecuted for misrepresentation of the facts and the application was finally refused with a confirmatory faculty being granted in its stead (see the previous paragraph). This decision was taken as the chancellor concluded that the site was previously 'a useless eyesore, an unsafe slum of an open space' and not, as objectors described it, 'a sacred site'.

The final judgement heard at the Diocese of London Consistory Court was made in 2017 and it is documented in a lengthy transcript (497 pages) entitled *In the matter of a building in the churchyard of Christ Church Spitalfields* and *In the matter of an application for a restoration order and a petition for a confirmatory faculty*.

The crux of the problems lay in a litany of errors within the faculty application process, which the chancellor said brought it into disrepute. It all started with the applicants failing to ascertain the true status of the land (stating that it was not consecrated when it was) and the previous chancellor failing to check this detail. The faculty application lacked attention to detail and was bedevilled by lost or missing documents, supposedly held safely by the relevant local authorities, and there were others that were unsigned. It also came to light that Muslim children were being taught at the school, contrary to Muslim religious principles preventing them from being in a building over any burial ground and particularly one where Christians are buried. Parents had not been made aware of this fact.

Much of the restoration work was funded by benefactors and this case is a stark warning to churches who rely on monies raised by active groups of 'friends', without giving sufficient thought to how these groups are organised or controlled and their legal relationship with the church they are seeking to help.

Playing your cards close to your chest - In 2016, a church in the Oxford diocese fell afoul of the faculty rules regarding the sale of church property, which resulted in the churchwardens having to appear before the Consistory Court to explain their actions. Two chests had been stored for some time and no use could be found for them. The PCC unanimously agreed to sell the items and sent them to auctioneers for disposal. The chests were only expected to raise £1,100, but they actually sold for £19,300. When this was found out, searches were made and a reference was found in the 1939 Oxford Inventory of the Royal Commission on Historical Monuments that established their antiquity. [23]

The rector promptly contacted the archdeacon, who suggested that the parish consult the diocesan registrar to seek a retrospective faculty 'to confirm authority for the sale, or purported sale' of the chests. The diocesan registrar wrote to the auctioneers highlighting that, as no faculty had been obtained for the sale, no ownership of the chests could be passed to the purported purchasers. The diocesan chancellor further advised that those who had facilitated the disposal of church goods had a responsibility to satisfy themselves that those responsible for selling the goods had the authority to do so. The churchwardens told the court that they did not wish the chests to be returned as they were of no practical use and no-one had expressed any particular attachment to them. The chancellor advised that it was of the utmost importance that heritage was conserved, regardless of whether it was perceived to be of practical use or whether any person had a particular attachment to it.

The chancellor considered reporting the matter to the bishop, so that he might censure the churchwardens over their conduct. However, in light of the churchwardens' extreme regret and ongoing embarrassment he felt it was unnecessary to do so, believing that they had learned a very salutary lesson, and the burden of costs in the case would inevitably fall on them.

In the light of this decision, the chancellor further decided that the court should not ask the archdeacon to institute a complaint of misconduct against the incumbent under the Clergy Disciplinary Measure 2003. The petition was withdrawn, but on stringent conditions. He ordered that the incumbent, PCC and churchwardens continue to pursue all reasonable avenues to identify the location and the current possessors of the two chests, and formally report to the court the attempts that they had made to make such identifications. Until further order of the court, the monies received for the chests were to be invested at the direction of the diocesan registrar. The churchwardens were ordered to pay the costs of the court proceedings.

Fingers crossed - In 2016, an ancient church (1180) in Leicestershire received £140,000 from the Heritage Lottery Fund to carry out essential repairs to the church and to part-convert it into a heritage centre dedicated to the lost medieval village that had once thrived there. However, there was a stipulation requiring that some kind of sign be erected stating the source of the money that had somehow been overlooked at the time of the faculty application. Having spent the money, St Bartholomew's Church in Welby retrospectively submitted a faculty to the diocese for permission to put up a large blue plaque, complete with the lottery emblem and information about the funding. The diocesan chancellor refused to permit the mounting of a Heritage Lottery Fund plaque on an inside wall of the porch of the church. Whilst acknowledging the conditions of the grant, he advised that the plaque was 'large and tasteless' and there was little justification for it to appear in a 12th century church (Grade I listed). One has to support his point of view, given that the proposed plaque was of transparent Perspex with blue writing, complete with the lottery fund's logo of a smiling face and a hand with crossed fingers. The chancellor said (tinged with a little sarcasm and acrimony methinks), 'I believe the crossed fingers are indeed a remote Christian reference, indicating prayer, and suggesting that punters might pray to be lottery winners. But I do not expect that the Christian reference will be noted by many.' He went on to admonish them by saying that, 'The real purpose of the motif was presumably to encourage those who bought lottery tickets to hope that they might become rich... which was not a particularly Christian purpose.' The chancellor later agreed to a plaque in a compact form, but in black and white only. The smaller the plaque, the more acceptable it would be. [24]

Chapter 4

PREACHERS

In medieval England, most churches were decorated with wall paintings which were used as visual aids by the priest as a *Biblia Pauperum* (a 'poor man's Bible'), to illustrate Christianity to the largely illiterate congregation. Sadly, these wonderful works of art were covered up with white lime-wash during the Protestant Reformation and it was to be another 300 years before they saw the light of day again. The arrival of the Reformation in England found churches served by clergy who were largely untrained, incompetent, and unconcerned about the wellbeing – spiritual or material – of the congregations they were to serve. As an interim measure, a book of homilies was produced for ministers to read to the people, until they were capable of preaching and expounding the scriptures themselves. Homilies would be resurrected in the 21st century to overcome problems with boring sermons!

The word 'preaching' means to orally proclaim something; to deliver a message. *The Laws Respecting Parish Matters,* published in 1805, state that 'it is the duty of the churchwardens to see that every new preacher is properly qualified by licence by the bishop; and unless he produce such licence, they are not to *suffer* him to preach'.[25] Nowadays, a new parish priest is chosen by the 'patron', acting together with the bishop and two parish representatives appointed by the PCC (usually the churchwardens). However, things were handled somewhat differently in the 17th century, when the quality of preaching was high on the list of requirements for the incumbent. At this time, preachers often relied on the quality of their preaching and the approval of their congregation to assure their livelihood. The churchwardens of one London parish, eager to employ the best preacher available, established a selection process that forced their candidates to engage in a trial series of sermons that would be voted on by the parishioners.

From a grateful congregation? - *Near this place are interred the remains of Vashti Smith. In 40 years as churchwarden she never let the preacher go on for more than 10 minutes. Sadly missed.* Recent scientific studies suggest that human attention spans have reduced dramatically since the introduction of electronic 'devices'. Some even suggesting a figure of eight seconds – preachers take note!

Catholic archbishops have urged priests to prepare well and to think carefully about the content of their homilies, saying that delivering boring sermons is unjust to God and to churchgoers. A synod of bishops in 2008 was so concerned about matters concerning homilies that a homiletic directory was produced to support their preparation. In 2010, the Vatican recommended that Catholic clergy kept their sermons under eight minutes to cater for people who found it hard to concentrate for long periods. However, research that same year found that some Anglican clergy preach for as long as 42 minutes! Following this revelation, one senior Anglican bishop urged clergy to cut the length of services in an effort to reverse declining attendance. He went on to say that worship was too complicated and time-consuming, leaving people who are not regular churchgoers feeling confused and excluded. He suggested that services should be no more than 50 minutes and that clergy should make sure that sermons are not too long, agreeing that 'the brain can only take in what the seat can endure'. However, there is an argument for not directing clergy to preach short sermons because it is important for people to understand the Word of God to allow them to grow spiritually.

Many years ago, during my Methodist youth, one of our local lay preachers was one H. Cecil Pawson (a professor at Newcastle University) who later became President of the Methodist Conference. Whilst the prof's sermons were profound, they did however turn into theological marathons. Placing a clock opposite the pulpit was to no avail and despite his wife fining him one shilling per minute over an agreed time, this proved no discouragement ('I've started so I will finish!'). I've been told about one old Methodist church where the stewards set a whistling kettle on the coke stove (the only heating in the church) at the start of the sermon, to serve as both a time management aid to the preacher and an alarm clock to the slumbering congregation. Others would perhaps have suggested that a rendering of 'Sleepers awake!' may have done the trick, however after the initial jolt of Bach's music, Somnus and Hypnos would soon be calling.

An unscientific survey in 2010 (via Twitter) sought to establish the ideal length of a sermon. It recognised that there may be a gap in perceptions between ministers and laity, with some preachers preferring to preach longer but feeling constrained by schedules. However, among congregations, nobody reported that sermons were too short. There has been a suggestion that preachers should be asked to deliver their address whilst standing on one leg; should the other foot touch the floor then time is up! The ultimate epitaph? – "Sacred to the memory of Rev. John Spokes (1853 – 1921) whose sermons gave this congregation glimpses of what eternity was like." Conclusion – if you wish your sermons could be longer, you're probably the only one. As John Stott (the renowned Christian writer) commented, 'it doesn't matter how long you preach, it should feel *like* 20 minutes.'

Chapter 5

CONTROL OF THE CONGREGATION

In the past, churchwardens needed to ensure that parishioners came to church, behaved in an orderly way and took their hats off. They would record absentees from services, as well as those who had walked out the church or talked during service time. They issued fines to all absentees and late-comers.

Minor offences - 'Indecorous behaviour', such as not paying attention or talking during a sermon, may have been punished by using the indoor stocks. The first two joints of the index and middle fingers were bent and inserted into the stock, making them immoveable. In the 17th and 18th centuries, men, women and even children were sentenced to be whipped or flogged. They were tied to a post and whipped by the parish churchwarden who was paid to do it. [26]

Finger pillory at St Helen's Church, Ashby-de-la-Zouch. Jimfbleak, own work.

'Absentees' - We might assume that in times past all 'God fearing people' would be in church on Sunday, however this was not always the case. It was customary for the churchwardens to leave the church during the second reading and tour the pubs of the area, making a note of those not present at church or those who were working ('marking'), then return in time to hear the sermon. Absentees would later be fined for their transgressions however this was not carried out consistently. In extreme cases, people would be excommunicated!

The churchyard - The churchwardens were 'not to suffer any idle persons to abide either in the churchyard or the church-porch during the time of divine service, or preaching'. They were also required to ensure that no feasts, dinners or common drinking were kept, and that no peddlers set out wares in church porches or churchyards during service time, and they were to prevent boys from playing games and shouting during the divine solemnities.

CONTROL OF SEATING IN CHURCH

Churchwardens are, as entrusted officers of the bishop and in the interest of good order, charged with controlling seating in the church. An orderly person cannot be excluded on the grounds that the church is full if that person can stand in a part of the church without interfering with the conduct of the service. Churchwardens have the authority to ask (or tell) the congregation where to sit and are empowered to move people by 'moderate force' if they do not comply. In the past, churchwardens sometimes segregated men and women during services to prevent them talking, flirting, or even worse, sharing a kiss during the Peace!

There is no evidence of Christian churches having seating of any kind for at least the first 1,400 years or so of Christianity. Seating in churches didn't arrive until parishioners got bored enough to wish they were sitting down – that is, about the time of the Protestant Reformation. All the pews in a parish church are the common property of the parish and for *use in common* by the parishioners, who are all entitled to be seated, orderly and conveniently, so as to best provide for the accommodation of all. It was argued in the case of Fuller v Lane in 1825 that 'the distribution of seats [in church] rests with the churchwardens as the officers, and subject to the control of the ordinary [the bishop]. Neither the ministers nor the vestry have any right whatever to interfere with the churchwardens in seating and arranging the parishioners.'[27]

Churchwardens cannot lawfully prevent a person from attending a service, even if they honestly believe that the church is full. Today, they still only have the right (in statutory law as well as ecclesiastical law) to prevent anyone entering the church for any purpose other than worship. In the past, the churchwarden's conundrum was that their authority was limited to the distribution of seats. However, subsequent court cases have declined to speculate what should happen if the church becomes overcrowded. This illogical situation effectively deprived the churchwardens of the full ability to maintain order during service. Some parishioner may decide to stand in the pulpit, or at the altar, thus obstructing the service, yet the churchwardens would be powerless to restrain or remove them. Removal of such a person might result in both the churchwarden and the worshipper being prosecuted; the warden for denying entry and the worshipper for not attending church. Nowadays, churchwardens would perhaps cite health and safety as a valid reason for refusing people entry to church or sitting where they choose.

Pew Renting

James 2: 1-4 (NIV) says, 'My brothers and sisters, believers in our glorious Lord Jesus Christ must not show favouritism. Suppose a man comes into your meeting wearing fine clothes and a gold ring, followed by a poor man in filthy old clothes. If you show special attention to the man wearing fine clothes and say, "Here's a good seat for you," but say to the poor man, "You stand there" or "Sit on the floor by my feet," have you not discriminated among yourselves and become judges with evil thoughts?' Whether this was read or preached in medieval times is unknown. If it was, then it fell on deaf ears with little evidence of humility being shown.

The word 'pew' comes from the Latin *podium* (elevated place); a platform for the privileged.

For most of the Christian ages, there were no pews, nor much seating of any sort. Pews arrived in Christian churches around the 12th century. However, filling churches with pews was chiefly the invention of the later Protestant revolution that saw adoration replaced with sophistication.

The church records for St George's in Poynton, Cheshire, tell us that in 1881, the vicar announced in the church magazine that 'as soon as the bell has stopped, every seat, wherever it may be situated is entirely free and open to anybody. Those who wish for sittings to be appropriated to them should make application to the Wardens, stating the number of sittings required...' (Sounds like musical chairs!)

Throughout the centuries, pew renting has caused churchwardens multifarious problems as influential families have insisted that they be accommodated according to their status, ignoring Jesus's instruction in Luke 14: 10 (NIV) that 'when you are invited, take the lowest place, so that when your host comes, he will say to you, "Friend, move up to a better place." Then you will be honoured in the presence of all the other guests.' The practice could perhaps be considered the forerunner to the football box season ticket, with the poor being relegated to the occasional stone bench around the walls or at the base of the columns (the 'terraces'). The box pew was popular with families, providing privacy and allowing them to sit together. In the 17th and 18th centuries they might have had a raised back to keep out draughts and they may have been fitted with doors (sometimes locked), snobbishly adorned with the family name or perhaps the family crest. Box pews for the rich were often on a gallery with their own entrances. They might also have had windows, curtains and even fireplaces!

A decree at the Synod of Exeter in 1297, confirmed by a court judgment in 1612, stated that a church 'is dedicated and consecrated to the service of God, and is common to all inhabitants'. It was therefore the responsibility of the bishop to resolve the issue of seat ownership. Despite this, pews were still being unlawfully rented until 1970, with the collusion of churchwardens and clergymen. A force against reform came from the 'pew-openers' who earned money for attending the idle rich, and often fees from pew rents provided a good chunk of the clergy salaries. Subsequent seating reforms were therefore resisted vociferously.

The crux of the problem was that people had paid money for the pews and therefore they insisted that they owned them, even putting nameplates on them to state the fact. Perhaps one of the first signs of trouble was in 1596 when Elinor Burnett stepped into Alison Brown's pew at All Saints Church, Oxford, and bade that she 'give her elders and betters some room'. Mrs Brown refused to give way and replied that she did acknowledge her to be her elder, but not her better.

A choice of pew, made by rich parishioners, was rather idiosyncratic. At Llangattock Church in Carmarthenshire, Mrs Crawshay brought her dogs and had tea served on a table in her pew during the service. In 1696, Lord Ashburnham complained to the churchwardens at Ampthill in Bedfordshire that he could not take his family to church for lack of 'due and proper accommodation'. It was all very well for the churchwardens to think about shuffling the congregation around to seat them according to rank, but another thing to actually do it. As the incumbent lacked the courage to get involved, the churchwardens resolved the dilemma by allowing a galleried pew (approved by Sir Christopher Wren) to be erected and furnished with silk hangings and velvet-cushioned easy chairs. So comfortable was His Lordship when the eucharist was celebrated, that he refused to leave his plush splendour and approach the altar, forcing the rector to climb up to the pew and administer the eucharist to him in situ.[28] In other cases, fires were stoked in pews by snug owners oblivious to the disturbance that they were causing by this incensory!

The subject of pews has turned full circle and today there is a rush to remove them and replace them with more comfortable chairs or padded benches. Not so the pews at St Clement's in Old Romney, which retains its handsome Georgian box pews, painted in a tasteful shade of blush (pink) complemented with black edges and white highlights. This choice was following a request from a film company making a film based on the smuggling adventures of Dr Syn, the smuggler hero of the novels written by Russell Thorndike. St Clement's, like many churches in Kent during the early years of 21st century, is enduring an interregnum, no doubt looking for a vicar whose colour pallet matches the church décor!

PAX DOMINI SIT SEMPER VOBISCUM

Of all the service changes made in recent years, none has caused so much confusion and friction as sharing the Peace.[29] The official order of service requires the priest to announce 'the peace of the Lord be always with you' and the congregation replies 'and also with you'. Unfortunately, an optional extra is allowed: 'let us all offer a sign of peace'. But what? This suggests some physical contact which some may not be happy with, especially if you are a visitor or newcomer to church.

I can vouch for this having come to the Anglican tradition from Methodism (everything in moderation). The great St Paul does not offer clarity either. In Galatians 2: 9 (NIV) he says that the disciples 'gave to [him] and Barnabas the right hands of fellowship', yet many times elsewhere he advises Christians to greet one another with a holy kiss! (This is an ancient traditional Christian greeting, known as a 'brother kiss' among men or a 'sister kiss' among women.) Some congregations do not allow inter-gender holy-kissing, perhaps because in days past, churchwardens segregated men and women during services to prevent them talking, flirting, or even worse, sharing a kiss at the Peace!

Congregants of a sensitive, health-conscious, nature may worry that it is more than the Peace they are sharing and the more people contacted, the greater the danger of infection. Pope Benedict XVI advised some years ago that nothing is lost when the sign of peace is marked by a sobriety which preserves the proper spirit of the celebration, as, for example, when it is restricted to one's immediate neighbours. So how do we appease the staid Anglicans? Do we perhaps adopt the Vatican *Redemptionis Sacramentum*, which advises that each one give the sign of peace (in a sober manner) only to those who are nearest? We could cater for the quiet introverts like Richard Stilgoe and Peter Skellern's Mrs Beamish by perhaps creating a 'Peace-free zone' to escape the ensuing melee. ('Don't you dare shake hands with me, or offer signs of peace!') Or perhaps the churchwardens could revert to the good old traditions of years gone by and use their trusty staves to maintain peace and decorum?

Chapter 6

THE CHURCHWARDENS' STAVES

Tony showed the churchwarden's wand was just a trick – honest.

The symbol of the churchwarden's office is the stave (sometimes called a prodder or wand). It is both a liturgical symbol of office as well as an indication of standing, importance and authority. It is the duty of the churchwardens to maintain order and decorum inside the church and churchyard during services. The stave may be used to 'persuade' the removal of persons causing disturbances. Canon 19 of 1603 required churchwardens 'not to suffer any idle persons to abide either in the churchyard or church-porch'. Canon 28 further required the sending of non-parishioners back to their own churches and Canon 60 commanded that they should repel 'unauthorised preachers'. Similarly, vergers (protectors of the procession) carried a 'virge' (rod) to keep back animals or overenthusiastic crowds from the person they were escorting or perhaps to discipline unruly choristers!

Now mainly used for ceremonial purposes, in the past churchwardens' staves would have been sharp pointed sticks used as a disciplinary aid. A useful tool for managing unruly members of the congregation or drunks who came into the church or churchyard intent on causing disruption during services! Punishments for affray were severe;[30] if any person struck another with a weapon within the church or churchyard, they could be sentenced to have an ear cut off. If they had no ears (persistent offender?) they might be branded on the cheek with the letter 'F' (fray-maker or fighter) and excommunicated - well Jesus's advice in Mark 4:23 (NIV) would be fruitless as further reprimand!

Today, Canon E1(4) provides that the churchwardens shall maintain order and decency, especially during the time of divine service and to deal with any riotous, violent or indecent behaviour in the church or churchyard. The permission to chastise (or awaken?) parishioners has never actually been rescinded. Even today, churchwardens have the legal right and duty, with or without the help of the police, to arrest anyone misbehaving. This applies to both clergy and lay members alike however if the clergy upset the churchwardens, then the wardens may complain to the bishop, but they have no right to arrest clergy or prevent them from ministering. In recent years a stave fulfilled its medieval purpose and proved more than useful in deterring an intruder at St. Mary's Prescot on Merseyside.

Chapter 7

MISDEMEANOURS

CHURCHWARDENS AND CLERGY

Parish archives have masses of literature dating from 1500 onwards detailing rows, quarrels and even legal battles when incumbents have challenged the role of the churchwardens or they have tried to sell, borrow, give away or steal church property that they mistakenly thought of as theirs to dispose of as they wished. In the period following the Reformation, church administration became somewhat lax, as the following cases demonstrate.

So incensed was the Archdeacon of Suffolk, Humphrey Prideaux, that he was inspired to write (in 1692) to his subordinates whom he addresses like a true diplomat (despite his obvious displeasure):

> My worthy Brethren,
>
> The ignorance of Churchwardens as to the duties of their office, which they have been sworn to, making Visitations in a manner ineffectual, and also frequently causing great differences and disturbances at home among their neighbours, through the errors and mistakes which they run into, about the repairs of your Churches, and the levying of rates for the same; I have thought it necessary to draw up these directions for the preventing of the like mischiefs and

inconveniences for the future; and if you will join your endeavours with me so far, as out of this paper every year to inform and instruct your Churchwardens, that they may the better know their duty both in presenting such things as are amiss in your respective parishes, and also in repairing your Churches, I would then hope that sin might be more effectually corrected, and Churches so repaired, that the worship of God might be performed in them with that decency which is fitting, without making this matter a fire-brand of contention among you (as it too often happens) to the wasting of that Christian charity among your people, which it is one of the main duties of your Ministry to support and maintain among them. I pray God bless us all in our endeavours to promote his honour and glory in that holy function which he hath called us to, or imposed on them.

And I am,
Your affectionate Brother and Servant[31]

In Suffolk however, a more serious misdemeanour prompted action from the Commissary for the Archdeaconry of Bedford against the churchwardens of Knotting Parish Church in Bedfordshire. The case against them was that the rector, churchwardens and several parishioners had been caught cock-fighting in the church on Shrove Tuesday in the consecutive years from 1634 to 1637. The action took place in the chancel, where fighting cocks were brought thither and many people assembled to watch, bet and lay wagers with spectators who laughed and sported profanely abused the said consecrated place. Gates were subsequently erected below the chancel arch to prevent any recurrence of this base activity. [32]

In 1703, there was a long-standing dispute between the Rev. David Jones and the churchwardens of Marcham in Oxfordshire,[33] which started with the vicar accusing a London brewer called Felix Calvert of interrupting a sermon and sending ale into church to drink to his health with certain other persons. Jones roundly criticised the churchwardens, claiming (amongst other things) that they provided bread and wine for Communion which was substandard, being so full of filth and gravel that it was not fit for consumption.

In 1834, the village of Stoney Middleton became a parish in its own right.[34] The first vicar of St Martin's Church was a man of strong puritanical ideology and zeal who set about the restoration of the 15th century church fabric. Unfortunately, his enthusiasm got the better of him and somehow during the work most of the treasures were mislaid, including the font and a marble monument. (Where were the churchwardens?)

The people of St Martin's have a reputation of giving diligent and long service to the upkeep of the church. Many years ago, there was only one churchwarden who had to do everything himself. When it came to ringing the bells (three of them) he was not discouraged and, putting the third rope around his foot, he would ring all three bells at the same time!

Churchwardens must work in partnership with their incumbent, supporting, and sharing a mutual respect. There may be times however when relationships become strained though, I suspect, none so constantly and vociferously as at Hathern Parish Church in Leicestershire.[35] Their history is well documented with incidents involving clergy, parishioners, churchwardens and even the archdeacon and bishop becoming involved.

During the 19th century, the church experienced successive firebrand rectors both of whom experienced uncomfortable relationships with their parishioners and the courts. The Rev. Edward Thomas March Phillipps[36] was a well-loved churchman with private means from the family seat (Garendon Hall). Shortly after ordination aged 24, he took the living of Rector at Hathern. As a devoted member of the Bible Society he committed his whole life to the education of adults and children alike, both within the parish and afar. Both altruistic and enterprising he created soup kitchens, a parish library, allotments and a medical store that provided vaccinations. Sadly he had no interest in either vestry business, or parish politics preferring to leave these matters to others.

Village crime was seen as 'petty' compared with other local villages. It was the shenanigans of itinerant journeymen who distressed the Rector most, causing him to utter strong comments regarding their rowdy preoccupations with cockfighting and drunkenness. Dispassionately (and unwisely) he described the Village as "the original place spoken of in the book of Revelation (*18:2*), as the hold of every foul spirit, a cage full of every unclean and hateful beast."[37] This comment resulted in the village being dubbed 'wicked Hathern'. The Bible Society's obituary for the Reverend March Phillips read 'the church had no better pastor and the Bible Society no better friend'. Villagers considered him a saint.

The Reverend Edward Smythies succeeded his father-in-law as Rector. Educated at Emmanuel College, Cambridge, he was presented the living at Hathern by Mr. Charles March Phillipps, the Squire of Garendon. The antithesis of his predecessor, he suspected most people of being malevolent and he became irascible and cantankerous in the extreme. There are no excuses for the reverend's behaviour but he did have an unfortunate family life which might explain his demeanour. Eight children by his first wife, five of whom died in tragic circumstances and his wife died young. His time at Hathern was marked by a series of unsavoury events and court actions; these mainly involved disputes over his non-payment of bills. One prominent case involved him being accused of stealing 30-40 tons of granite, the subject of disputed ownership with Loughborough Highways Board. The intended use for the stone was to build dwellings in the village. After protracted deliberations, the judge found in favour of the rector. Despite this decision, the matter grumbled on for a total of six years, with the rector making spiteful and malicious machinations, threatening to sue the Highways should they deny him access to the stone.

Relations deteriorated between the rector and certain members of the vestry committee and at various times he was accused of libel and slander by using inflammatory language. There was also an incident of vote-rigging in the chosen churchwarden's suitability for office, alleging the nominee to be a nonconformist. Matters were raised with the archdeacon who severely admonished Reverend Smythies for his untruths. He further rebuked him for apportioning blame for his current problems to his predecessors' comments regarding village wickedness; thus exacerbating, rather than him seeking to improve, matters. Shortly after this, the Rev. Edward Smythies became seriously ill and died, leaving his successor, the Reverend Joseph Glen Lawrence, to pick up the pieces and restore parish relationships. It was Rev. Smythies children, not the parishioners, who installed a stained-glass memorial window in his memory. The funeral took place at Hathern Church; however, it was noticeable that no members of the vestry committee were present.

They say that you have to move with the times, constantly re-inventing yourself to stay relevant. The word 'wicked' has entered the urban dictionary and may now be used as a positive – 'wicked man!' – very good / awesome. Today, 'Wicked Hathern' is being used to promote an annual music festival and a new brewery with an ale called Cockfighter!

COURTING TROUBLE?

There were no police in medieval times. Crime was, to a great extent, controlled by the Church who introduced extreme punishments to hopefully keep people in order, by fear. As an additional deterrent, all people were encouraged to attend the courts so as to appreciate the punishments meted out; failure to do so was punished by a fine. Minor crimes would be dealt with by the manorial courts (trial by jury), where humiliation, stocks and pillories were the tools of punishment. More serious crime was dealt with by the King's Court, where guilt was determined by various 'trials' (in essence tortures) by the use of fire, water or combat to prove or disprove guilt. Survival of these trials proved your innocence but often left you scarred physically or mentally. Perhaps the courts referred to biblical texts when dealing with such matters. For example, 1 John 4: 1 (NIV) says 'do not believe every spirit but test the spirits to see whether they are from God'. When dealing with witches, surviving a ducking indicated that the woman was guilty, as God's water had rejected her. Conversely, if she drowned she was proven innocent! A lose-lose situation!

ECCLESIASTICAL COURTS

Courts Christian, or courts spiritual, dealt with a variety of matters presented to them by church officers and parishioners regarding disciplinary issues. The churchwardens concerned themselves with the morals of the community, dealing with a multitude of sins. For example, there were cases of blaspheming, failure to attend church, defamation, slander, unseemly behaviour in church, working or rowdy drinking on a Sunday, not having children baptised, simony (the buying or selling of ecclesiastical privileges such as pardons or benefices), heresy, witchcraft, usury (lending money at high rates of interest) 'criminous conversation' (adultery or fornication), incest and bearing a bastard. Indeed, it was the preoccupation with matters of morality that caused the ecclesiastical courts to be known as the 'courts of scolds' or 'bawdy courts'.

Ecclesiastical courts also heard cases of land disputes, probate matters, breaches of promise and other matrimonial matters including separation and divorce. Appearances before a court were so common that some dioceses prepared 'statements of penance', leaving spaces for the names of the guilty party to be written in.

Chapter 8

INVOLVEMENT OF THE CHURCHWARDENS IN CIVIL DUTIES

The parish clerk (or town clerk) - From the beginning of the third century there is evidence of clerks in minor orders and they are mentioned in a letter written by Pope Gregory to Augustine at the start of the seventh century. In early times, these clerks went under the Latin name *Aquae Bajulus* (holy water bearer) and at their induction, they received an aspergillum (holy water sprinkler) which they used every Sunday to go around the parish and dust everyone with holy water. Usually chosen by the priest, they were young, with a vision to be a priest themselves (clerks in minor orders were considered to be 'apprentices' to the priest). Post-Reformation, the parish clerk's duties were redefined and the 'minor orders' were removed (demoted), making them lay officers who attended every church service, keeping people awake and collecting pew rents.

Official parish registers - These were first introduced by Henry VIII and Thomas Cromwell to record births, marriages and deaths. Prior to that date, informal records existed but they only related to leading local families. Records of Sunday worship would also be kept, written down in the presence of the churchwardens. By 1597, it was a requirement to keep registers in books and the parish clerk had to copy the old records into a new parchment book, keeping the records up-to-date and sending copies to the bishop's registrar. If the churchwardens or overseers were illiterate, the parish clerk wrote their accounts for them, listing church rates and assisting officers in their collections of tolls for sheep pastured in the churchyard, or for those who hung their washing there or set up stalls along the church path on market days. By using the parish clerk, most parishes managed to sustain a uniform pattern of accounting.

Dog whippers - Any sentence starting with the words 'they say' is usually hearsay; rarely true. So it may be with the celebration of 'Whip-Dog Day' on St Luke's Day, 18 October. The tradition, dating back many centuries, supposedly began with a priest accidentally dropping a eucharist wafer whilst celebrating mass on that particular festival day. The wafer was snapped up and eaten by a dog who was promptly killed, dooming their future brethren to flagellation in memory of the sacrilege. I doubt whether there is any truth in this tale, which was probably concocted in order to justify the need for churchwardens to employ dog whippers to deal with the many dogs who found their way into churches and howled at the hymns!

Parishes appointed a paid dog whipper (knocknobbler[38] an Elizabethan expression) to keep dogs [and unruly children?] out of church, particularly sheepdogs which farmers habitually took into services. It has even been suggested that altar rails were built at a certain height and enclosed to exclude dogs from the sanctuary. Dog whippers[39] carried a whip and used tongs, either of wood or iron, which fastened around the animal's neck. There is a dog whipper's pew preserved in St Margaret's Church in Wrenbury, Cheshire. At St Anne's Church, Baslow and Bubnell, Derbyshire, there is a glass case inside the church by the door, displaying a dog whip that some historians claim was also used to maintain order among worshippers, awakening those who snored during the service.

Dog whippers were common in Tudor times with references to them as 'forristors of ye doggs' who were paid for 'jacking ye dogs.' The role became less common from the late 18th century and the last record of a dog whipper being employed was John Pickard, appointed 'bearer of the dog whipper's rod' at Exeter Cathedral in 1856. It might be perhaps assumed that the dog whipper was more important than the churchwardens, as a room in the cathedral (still known as the dog whipper's flat) was provided for his use. The room, high up within the walls of the cathedral, had an upper bedroom and below was a living room complete with fireplace and bread oven which looked down onto the nave. The custom died out in the late 19th century when animal welfare became more prominent. No evidence of it survives today, unless the street 'Whip-Ma-Whop-Ma-Gate' in York is related to the practice. It has also been suggested that dogs were used in the sanctuary to protect the valuable chalices, ciboria and crosses, etc.

Parish surveyors of the highways - These were appointed annually from 1555 (lasting for around 300 years) and sometimes known as waywardens. They were under the jurisdiction of the Justices of the Peace and chosen from people who owned 'estate'. Served with a warrant by the parish constable confirming their appointment, acceptance was compulsory. 'The Constables and Churchwardens of every Parish, shall yearly upon Tuesday or Wednesday in Easter Week, call together some of their Neighbours, and then make choice of two within the Parish, to be Surveyors of the High-Ways the Year following, who shall forthwith take that Office upon them, in pain to forfeit 20 s. apiece. The said Constables and Churchwardens shall then also nominate four days betwixt that time and Midsummer, to be set apart for the amendment of the High-ways, and shall give public notice thereof in the Church the next Sunday after Easter'.

Whilst surveyors could levy a rate for the upkeep of roads and ask any employer to supply labourers for up to two weeks per year, they themselves could also be fined for refusing to accept office or neglecting their duty. It was the job to be avoided at all costs. Surveyors were responsible for the parish roads, lanes and drainage ditches, and throughout the medieval period, the main users of the highways were pack animals, horses, herds of cattle, heavy carts and wagons. Quarterly, the surveyor would have to appraise all the roads, byways, water courses and pavements within his precinct and make a sworn presentation of his findings to the Justices of the Peace. If defects could be attributed to any particular person, then the surveyor was required to stand up in the parish church and identify the offender so that they might be prosecuted.

Watchmen - What did the Romans do for us? Well, perhaps they were the originators of health and safety principles. Hygeia (the daughter of Aesculapius, the god of medicine) was the goddess of health, cleanliness, and sanitation, and Salus was the Roman goddess of safety and well-being. Hygiene and safety. Coroners' reports rom the 16th and 17th centuries show that these were dangerous times, with half of all fatal accidents happening in 'the workplace'. In response, our Tudor ancestors were risk-aware and issued instructions covering vital issues such as how to mow hay, collect water, climb trees and kill wildlife. They produced a document entitled *Five Hundred Points of Good Husbandry*, which featured rhyming couplets warning of the many dangers of everyday life. Copies would have been found in almost every parish in England. The measures, rudimentary by today's standards, demonstrated an effort to minimise risks. Similar 'couplets' are still around today: 'when in doubt, check it out', 'protect your head or end up dead', 'a little care makes accidents rare', etc...[40]

Houses in the middle ages were made of wood, of haphazard design and questionable construction. Built close together with candle lighting, cooking was done on open fires and tradesmen used large ovens, kilns and forges. Fire risk was high. In 1200, laws were passed banning thatched roofs and in 1620, a new order was made stating that new buildings should be made from brick or stone and that top floors should not jut out into the street. Towns appointed inspectors (council building inspectors) to check houses for fire hazards and they would issue fines if people had not made their property safe. Watchmen were employed by local communities to patrol the streets at night and it was their job to guard against fire in hot weather, advising householders to leave buckets of water outside their doors.

The Great Fire of London in 1666 resulted in churchwardens in all parishes being required (by law) to ensure that a hand-operated fire engine and a leather pipe were kept ready for any such emergencies. A year later, the first proper insurance company was set up, appropriately called Phoenix. It was established by Dr Nicholas 'If-Christ-had-not-died-for-thee-thou-hadst-been-damned' Barbone, who was instrumental in the rebuilding of London. The good doctor was a Puritan financial speculator and his altruism in this venture was doubted by some. His unusual middle name, an example of a hortatory name, was given to him by his strongly Puritan father. Religious 'slogan names' were often given in Puritan families in 17th-century England. Nicholas was the eldest son of 'Praise-God' Barebone (or Barbon), after whom the Barebone's Parliament of 1653 was named, the predecessor of Oliver Cromwell's Protectorate.

The Factory Inspectorate was formed in 1833 and for the first 60 years it employed only male inspectors. Alexander Redgrave, the Chief Inspector of Factories (another chauvinist), was opposed to the introduction of women inspectors. He stated in his annual report of 1879, 'I doubt very much whether the office of factory inspector is one suitable for women. The general and multifarious duties of an inspector of factories would really be incompatible with the gentle and home-loving character of a woman'. It took another 140 years before the Health and Safety at Work Act (HASWA) was introduced, followed a year later by the formation of the Health and Safety Executive.

The PCC can be considered as the church management committee and it is a legal entity under health and safety law. Whilst PCCs have a duty of care for all people visiting church premises, they have no responsibility under the HASWA for risks created by the work activity of others, such as those maintaining the buildings, or for the activities organised by those who use the premises. As custodians of the church fabric however, churchwardens should satisfy themselves that third parties have taken appropriate risk assessments to ensure safe practices.

Surgeons - This is a somewhat misrepresentative name suggesting some degree of professionalism, but surgeons were not always supported by any formal qualifications (quack-salvers). Surgeons in the early part of the middle ages were often monks because they had access to the best medical literature (often written by Arab scholars). But in 1215, Pope Innocent III directed monks (clergy) to stop practising surgery and suggested that peasants should be instructed to perform various forms of surgery instead. This meant that farmers, who had little experience other than castrating animals, were in demand to perform anything from removing a painful tooth, to treating abscesses and performing more serious surgery. Later, things marginally improved with the introduction of licenced members of the Guild of Barber Surgeons (the GPs and dentists of their day). Barber surgeons would normally have been apprenticed to a more experienced associate, although few would have any formal learning and were often illiterate. Blood-letting was their speciality, as well as extracting teeth, giving enemas, 'dispensing' medicines, and, of course, cutting hair and trimming beards. In 1745, King George II established the London College of Surgeons, making surgeons university educated.

Scavengers - No, these are not the folk who man the bric-a-brac stall at the autumn fair, but people who would be appointed by the constable and churchwardens by virtue of a warrant from the Justice of the Peace. These (unpaid) inhabitants were known as master scavengers and performed their duties in return for payment of poor relief and parish favour. The scavenger would tour the parish six days a week (not Sunday), sweeping the streets and removing any dirt and detritus to a safe place. They would be fined if they failed to do so. There were also self-employed scavengers who were in essence 'recyclers', gathering bones to make into glue or rags, and wood and metal to sell or to strike private deals with householders to make money.

Parish (or petty) constables - The petty constable was a local official whose origins date back to Anglo-Saxon times. The equivalent of today's police 'specials', they were the eyes and ears of the Justices of the Peace and they were supervised by the churchwardens. Elected from respectable tradesmen, craftsmen and shopkeepers (not ordinary labourers), they were unpaid and served for one year only. Most parish constables did not wear a uniform and their only identifiable feature was the staff or truncheon they carried. Their role was thankless and arduous; they sometimes had to report the criminous activities of friends and neighbours. If they were caught turning a blind eye, they themselves risked being disciplined.

The constable had a comprehensive list of responsibilities and tasks that included: collecting miscellaneous rates and taxes; licencing inns and managing trading standards; managing weights and measures; and even controlling building regulations. They apprehended criminals and took them to court, escorted paupers on their journey to their place of settlement, and maintained the pillories, stocks and the gaol.

As they were regulated by an Act of Charles II, the constables became known as 'Charleys'; a name that would later ignominiously describe their demeanour. As crime rates rose during the Victorian era, the constables were proving ineffective in many areas to such an extent that they were often depicted as figures of fun or irresponsible drunkards, little better than those they were arresting.

Until 1894, it was the churchwardens' duty to control and pay the local militia, provide chests to store weapons and watch over the stock of the 'towne armes' that were kept in the church for the militia to use in an emergency! There are at least two cases recorded at the National Archives of churchwardens calling out the militia, arming them, sending them into the church to arrest the incumbent, then handing him over to the bishop.

LAW AND ORDER

Whilst parish churches relied on their churchwardens to maintain law and order, since the 13th century, cathedrals have appointed their own ecclesiastical constables. After a suspected arson at York Minster in 1829, the Chapter established a minster police force. Today, along with Liverpool, Canterbury and Chester, the cathedral still employs such officers. They keep staff and visitors safe and secure, and still retain a power of arrest under Section 3 of the Ecclesiastical Courts Jurisdiction Act 1860, with respect to disruptive behaviour within a cathedral church and its precincts. Their Latin motto, *In Deo Speramus*, means simply 'In God We Trust'.[41]

During the early 1960s, I was a steward (sidesman) at Denton Burn Methodist Church in Newcastle upon Tyne. During this dawn of electronic technology, transistors were soon to revolutionise solid state electronics, but they did initially suffer some bugs in the system. Our stewardship meeting (PCC) was taking a leap of faith, having made the bold decision to acquire an electronic organ to replace the trusty old piano. Whilst the organ console was no larger than the piano it replaced, the wall mounted speaker was about the size of a 2-seater sofa! All went well, until one Sunday morning when we heard an urgent voice bellow from the speaker: 'Z victor one to delta two. Come in Z victor one; state your location!' Whilst the message was not preceded by a burst of Johnny Todd (Z-Cars theme – the euphemism for Mr Plodd), it was immediately apparent that the police VHF radios were breaking through our amplifier. Just as well they were polite and discrete and did not share any intimate details of criminal activity.

Similar problems occurred when radio microphones began to be introduced . When I was churchwarden , a funeral was interrupted by breakthrough from an adjacent church where a WI meeting was in progress - Jerusalem was not the funeral party's chosen hymn, so it was fortunate that a quick fix was made to address the problem before the WI meeting's grand finale. The final resolve required some delicate conversations - "Your equipment is faulty", "no it's not it's yours", etc. etc. etc.

Chapter 9

FINANCIAL MANAGEMENT

Past churchwardens were responsible for setting and collecting the church rate, and they were called upon to sit on various charitable committees and to administer bequests to the church. Along with the overseers, they administered education and managed parish relief by seeing that the poor law was properly applied (originally the churchwardens were also the overseers).

TITHES

Tithes, earlier known as 'frith-bohr' (a peace-pledge) were originally a payment-in-kind, such as crops, wool or milk. They were part of an agreed proportion of the yearly profits from farming, paid by parishioners, for the support of their parish church and clergy. Peasants worked for free on church land, making it difficult for them to work their own plots and produce food for their families.

The fourth-century decrees of Pope Gelasius had stipulated the use of tithes – a tax at the rate of one tenth of all goods and produce on land. This would be done through a system of quadripartition – a division between the bishop, clergy, the poor, and the church fabric. However, the bishops soon became aware that the monasteries were hijacking the monies for their own properties. To prevent many parish churches from falling into disrepair, 13th-century bishops issued orders to rectify the problem. These episcopal statutes introduced the principle of parishioners paying for the maintenance of the nave, whilst the rector would bear the costs for the upkeep of the chancel.

The medieval Church dominated everybody's life, be they village peasants or townspeople. People believed that Heaven and Hell existed as well as God, and from birth they were taught that the only way they could get to Heaven was if the Roman Catholic Church let them. The Church's control over the people was absolute and they were told of the terrors awaiting them if they failed to attend church. They were coerced into paying the tithe on the premise that their souls (on death) would go to Hell if they failed to do so.

THE CHURCH RATE

This was a contentious issue and remains so today in some parts of the world where baptism automatically registers them as a member of a church, thus making them compulsorily liable for payment of a church rate based on a percentage of their annual income. Renouncing membership is an option, but it comes at a price.

The church rate was an assessment of the notional annual rental value of a property, with each parish levying a different rate. Establishing the exact level of taxation at the start of the year was virtually impossible, given that the variances in the cost of living, the exigencies of the weather, illness, and the 'characters' of the overseers and churchwardens could all influence the level of expenditure. The rate was decided by the vestry meeting and collected by parish rate collectors.

The whole parish paid for the upkeep of the church and its parish, irrespective of their religious beliefs. Clergy were not exempt from payment. Every parishioner who contributed to the church rate (or the 'scot and lot' as it was referred to) had the right to attend the vestry meetings. Brewer's Dictionary of Phrase and Fable (1898) defines 'scot and lot' as 'a levy on all subjects according to their ability to pay'. 'Scot' means a tribute or tax, and the 'lot' is the allotment or portion assigned. To pay 'scot and lot' was therefore to pay the personal tax allotted to you. Conversely, not to pay was to get off 'scot-free'. However, by the late 18th century, it became more difficult to collect the rate from those who did not attend church and the collection was frequently complicated by conscious objections.

Conscious objections - There were objections from non-Anglicans (see chapters 13 and 14), not just on grounds of religious belief but also on principle. The Church of England received financial support from the government, whilst other denominations were dependent on voluntary contributions. Appeals against the value set on an individual house that determined whether the owner or occupier should pay (or 'pleas of poverty') all had to be heard by a Justice of the Peace, who was charged with overseeing the probity of the claims. Those who defaulted were fined.

Matters came to a head in 1836 with the formation of the Church Rate Abolition Society, which was formed to coordinate the activities of local objectors and resulted in concessions being made to the non-conformists. Finally, in 1868, the Compulsory Church Rates Abolition Act was passed, removing compulsory rates and making them voluntary. As of May 2012, the Act was still on the Statute Book, making it possible for PCCs to continue to levy voluntary rates by virtue of the Parochial Church Councils (Powers) Measure of 1956. As an example, in 1986, Hampstead Parish sought to raise a 'voluntary rate' in order to redecorate the interior of their Georgian Church.[42] Because the response from the parishioners, on that occasion, was positive, they have continued to raise the rate each year since, purely for building maintenance. Based on council tax bandings, it is equivalent to £0.01 for each £1 of council tax.[42]

CHAPTER 10

SETTLEMENT AND THE POOR LAW

(SOCIAL SERVICES)

A poor law system was first mooted in 1388, in an attempt to address labour shortages following the Black Death in England, which had restricted the mobility of labourers. These poor laws specified that each parish must look after its poor and that one third of the tithe and alms collections were supposed to go towards sustaining the poor of the parish.

The Poor Relief Act 1662 (an 'Act for the Better Relief of the Poor of this Kingdom'), also known as the Settlement and Removal Act, was introduced in response to the increasing numbers of beggars and vagrants. Its purpose was to establish to which parish a person belonged and thereby clarify who was responsible should poor relief be required. This was the first time that a document to prove a person's domicile had become statutory. It was known as a 'settlement certificate'. If anyone wished to move to another parish, then they needed to obtain this document and take it with them; similar to a modern identity card or passport.

Over the 351 years since the first complete code of poor relief was introduced, to its abolition in 1948, it was extremely contentious. Its application relied heavily on parish administration, which was invariably managed by unpaid, non-professional people who were trying to meet the needs of the poor whilst having to satisfy the demands of the avaricious rate payers. The system was intended to provide a benefit for those who fell on hard times, however it was deviously and voraciously manipulated by employers who were keen to reduce their financial commitment towards the relief fund. A 1665 amendment to the Act attempted to give transparency to the process by requiring incomers to the parish to register with the relevant authorities (the churchwardens or overseers). Those responsible had to publish arrival registrations in the local church Sunday circular and announce them to the congregation. Despite this, the conniving continued.

Poor relief was funded by a levy on leaseholders and freeholders (employers) in the parish and augmented by charities who would distribute free material to make sheets and clothing. Most of what we would now consider as 'social services' was provided by religious institutions: they gave temporary housing and food handouts (similar to food banks) to the poor, disabled or aged. They cared for the sick and provided education and sanctuary for the vulnerable. Adam Smith (a Scottish economist) was unsympathetic to the plight of the poor. In 1776, in his published paper *An Inquiry into the Nature and Causes of the Wealth of Nations*, he suggested that those unable to work should be allowed to fend for themselves, and starve if necessary. No relief should be given. During the 19th century, workhouses increasingly became a refuge for the elderly, infirm and sick, rather than the able-bodied poor.

Whilst all this support sounds altruistic, a good deal of services (including medical) were provided by workhouses. Ironically, these later became hospitals, and later still, they were converted into local authority care homes after the introduction of the 1948 National Assistance Act.

Churchwardens would meet monthly with the overseers of the parish to manage the relief of the poor. However, tight budgets, devious rate-payers and personal relationships with benefit recipients resulted in the system not being applied consistently or with equanimity. Churches began to distinguish the 'worthy' poor from the 'unworthy poor'. They favoured helping the upper-class wealthy people who had lost their income but were too ashamed to beg, over those who continued to beg, who they considered to be too lazy and unworthy to receive charity. Some people found it difficult to 'swallow their pride' and submit themselves for examination, whilst others, the 'professional poor', were ingenious in feigning disabilities and enhancing their petition when describing their misfortunes. They acquired black-market certificates and claimed benefits from multiple sources.

The poor relief assessment - All people of the parish were first assessed to establish their status as bona-fide parishioners (a settlement examination). Successful people would receive a 'certificate of settlement'. Following that initial test, they would then be measured against strict criteria to establish whether they were (or not) capable of work and eligible for financial relief from the parish rate. Parishioners were categorised as:

Poor by impotency - These people were aged, decrepit, lame, blind, mentally impaired, infants, etc. They would be granted relief and allowance.

Poor by casualty - These people were maimed, 'undone by fire', or 'overcharged' with children. If they were 'of ability and strength', they would be set to work by the overseers and further 'relieved' as necessary. Employers were encouraged by churchwardens to accept children between the ages of 7 and 15 as pauper apprentices, until they were aged 24 for men, or 21 for women. Many poor people were given false hope, viewing apprenticeships as an opportunity towards skilled work. Employers, however, often saw them as an opportunity for cheap labour and provided them with menial tasks such as domestic service or agricultural labour. Adult males were enthusiastic as they were excused from military service and they were guaranteed to receive a settlement certificate. Others who were unable to support themselves were offered accommodation and employment in the workhouse.

Poor by rioting, idleness, drunkenness, etc. - This group received no relief (except in extreme circumstances) and they would be sent to a house of correction where they would be subject to beatings and hard labour to help them realise the error of their ways. *'The floggings will continue until performance improves!'*

Those granted relief - They were not treated sympathetically, as they were required to wear a badge on their right sleeve, displaying a large letter 'P' and the first letter of their parish. Failure to do this would result in a fine and they would possibly be sent to the house of correction.

Absconders - The *Poor Law Unions' Gazette* (1856-1903)[43] was a weekly publication in which churchwardens and overseers published information in an attempt to trace paupers from all over the country who had deserted, leaving their wives and families chargeable to the poor law unions. The authorities, not wishing to be saddled with the responsibility of financially providing for such families, issued descriptions of the deserters to facilitate their apprehension. 'Advertisements' were often very detailed and colourful. Sometimes rewards were offered for any information leading to the apprehension of absconders (attracting bounty hunters).

Poor Clergy

Clergy were paid a salary (stipend) from the parish tithes. However, by the turn of the 17th century, the problem of poor clergy was becoming acute. The Church of England had been stripped of its assets and been drained of resources by successive grasping monarchs and gentry since the first days of the Reformation. Widespread clerical poverty was handicapping the work of the Church, with many clergy taking on additional jobs to supplement their income, thereby neglecting their parishes. In 1704, a solution arrived in the form of the Queen Anne's Bounty Act (for the 'augmentation of the maintenance of the poor clergy'). The Queen agreed to write off the debts of poorer clergy and she granted support from a compulsory clergy tithes fund (later augmented by large parliamentary deposits), which was used to increase their salaries.

Pensions

Pensions were another contentious issue, creating a clear social divide among parishes. From the late 1730s, parishes accepted substantial donations from wealthier residents in exchange for annuities for their widows. Whilst money collected after divine service (alms) was meant to provide ongoing support for 'only the most deserving of "decayed" householders', it rarely did, often finding its way to the better off rather than those who needed it most.

Chapter 11

BEATING THE BOUNDS

Before the introduction of maps, the annual (ancient) tradition of 'beating the bounds' or 'perambulations' was used as a method of reaffirming the parish boundaries. It is still observed in some English and Welsh parishes. Knowing the boundaries of the parish was crucial to a community's identity and they were usually marked by stones and later by metal plaques. It is alleged that the tradition of beating the bounds has its roots in the ancient Roman festival of Terminalia, which celebrated the Roman god Terminus, who ruled over boundaries. His appearance was like that of a stone, hence the stone boundary markers used in England. The custom of 'gangdays', on which people went 'a-ganging', had been kept since before the Norman Conquest, with religious ceremonies taking place on Ascension Day, or during Rogation Week, in May. Before the advent of maps, it was usual to make a formal 'perambulation' of the parish boundaries, recording the limits of each parish to prevent people from moving parish without permission, to establish their liability to contribute to the repair of the church and to confirm their right to be buried within the churchyard. The parish priest, along with the churchwardens and other church officials, would head a group armed with green boughs (usually birch or willow) who 'beat the parish', sharing their knowledge of where the boundaries lay, all the while praying for protection and blessings for the lands during the coming year. Hymns would be sung and often Psalms 103 and 104 were recited ('Praise the Lord, oh my soul'). The priest would declare, 'Cursed is he who transgresseth the bounds or doles of his neighbour.' (Not good for inter-parish relations.)

The 'celebrations' included punishments and sacrifices carried out so that people would remember where the boundaries lay. In particular, children were bounced on their heads at strategic points to 'fix these matters in their minds'! In more recent times, the process was one of carrot and stick, or more accurately, stick and carrot. The beating party carried birch sticks to inflict various 'punishments' (all in the best possible taste of course) and the day ended with a celebratory party. In England, a parish ale was always held after the perambulation, which assured the event's popularity. In Henry VIII's reign, the occasion had become an excuse for so much revelry that it attracted the condemnation of one preacher, who declared, 'these solemne and accustomable processions and supplications be nowe growen into a right foule and detestable abuse.'

In Manchester in 1597, John Dee recorded in his diary that he, with the curate, the clerk and the 'diverse of the town of diverse ages' perambulated the bounds of the parish, taking six days in all. In 2017

Chester diocese suggested that following the success of "Back to Church Sunday", many parishes were considering using a 'beating the bounds' event as an opportunity for community activities.

A good example of the benefits of 'beating the bounds' as a means of managing the poor law occurred in 1802 in Beaulieu, Hampshire, at the boundary line with Boldre in the New Forest. My four-times grandfather John Cruit and his relatives lived on a straggling, illegal and enigmatic settlement which had grown up along an earth bank adjacent to Beaulieu Manor, part of the New Forest, owned by the crown. The majority of the inhabitants were living in poverty, scavenging to make a living. They were described in the parliamentary papers of the 1830s as 'for the most part smugglers and deer-stealers' (and peat stealers). In those days, the New Forest was a lawless area where all levels of society were in some way involved in smuggling. Even the local church and Beaulieu Abbey were at times used to store contraband.

Manors usually provided housing for their workers, but Beaulieu Manor did not. It left the housing responsibility to the parish of Boldre, where parish and parishioners unwittingly benefitted each other through their independent actions. The parishioners, having commandeered land, had been allowed to build mud and cob cottages, thus relieving the parish of the need to do so. Meanwhile, the parish had bought land and put the poor to work to earn their keep, thus circumventing their need to implement the poor law arrangements. A blind eye was turned to these unusual arrangements, but manorial disputes arose as to where the actual boundary line lay and which parish would bear responsibility for the inhabitants should they ever require poor relief. At first, Beaulieu parish officers were unsympathetic to the plight of the parishioners and sought legal intervention. This was expensive, and the cost of evicting encroachers often exceeded the value of the land. Before long, arbitration by a barrister was agreed and his recommendation was that officers of both parishes involved would perambulate the bounds of Boldre and Beaulieu according to the line that the barrister had laid down. This was to be done every year. After the initial perambulation, out of the 50 properties concerned in the dispute, 13 were agreed to be Beaulieu's responsibility and the remaining 37 would belong to Boldre. Some pieces of encroached land could not be shown to belong to the crown, so discretion was exercised, with the result that some settlers became freeholders whilst others became tenants.

Chapter 12

SOCIAL FUNDRAISERS
Keep calm, it's Beer O'Clock

Probably the most enjoyable part of being churchwarden!

Benjamin Franklin is often credited with the quote 'beer is proof that God wants us to be happy'. However, this is a corruption of his original quote: 'Behold the rain which descends from heaven upon our vineyards, there it enters the roots of the vines, to be changed into wine, a constant proof that God loves us, and loves to see us happy.' Amen!

This misquote has a certain truth, inasmuch that our ancestors took every opportunity to indulge in frequent and copious tastings. Sumerian writings dating back to 2500BC contain references to beer, and the *Hymn to Ninkasi* served as both a prayer and a method of remembering the recipe for beer, in a culture with few literate people.[44]

Every loaf of bread is a tragic tale of a cluster of grains that could have become a beer but didn't.[45] In 1868, James Death (a former brewer at Egypt's Cairo Brewery) put forward a theory in his book *The Beer of the Bible* that the manna from heaven that God gave the Israelites was a bread-based, porridge-like beer called *wusa*. In the 17th century, monks in strict orders adhered to a liquid-only fast[46] during lent, consuming no solids. To sustain them during this time they turned to a staple of the period – beer. They brewed a beer high in carbohydrates and nutrients, copying the oldest-surviving beer recipe, and in doing so they made 'liquid bread' that would not break their fast. Not wishing to fall foul of the Pope, they requested his blessing and to prove that drinking beer for 40 days wasn't a pleasure, they sent a barrel of beer from Munich to the Vatican. As the barrel traversed the Alps through the heat of Italy, it sloshed around and by the time it reached Rome it had soured and was undrinkable. After due consideration, the Pope decided that drinking the libation could actually build character, making the monks humbler, so he allowed them to continue the practice.

The rule of St Benedict stated that each monk be prescribed half a litre of wine per day. However, its advice was 'let us agree at least as to the fact that we should not drink till we are sated, but sparingly.' Proverbs 20: 1 (NIV), 'wine is a mocker and beer a brawler; whoever is led astray by them is not wise'.

It has been said that, along with the vicar and churchwarden , the landlord was one of the most important people in a village . Whilst pubs are now known as public houses, many started off as a room in someone's home. As seating space became a problem, the church was the most obvious place to congregate (until the Reformation) and the two co-existed as happy bedfellows . Religious houses through the ages have continued brewing to support themselves financially and this has perhaps flavoured some of the beer names seen today: Bishops Finger, from the finger-shaped signposts that pointed pilgrims on their way to the tomb of Thomas à Becket in Canterbury; Reverend James, named after Rev. James Buckley, one of the original owners of Buckley Brewery; and Churchyard Bob, from when method ringers used the term 'Churchyard Bob' to signal the crossover of bell ringers. Tiddly Vicar and Thirsty Monk require no qualification, and recently a Canadian brewer has finally introduced a beer named Churchwarden. Cheers!

Church houses - Beat Kümin,[47] professor of Early Modern European History at the University of Warwick, is the author of *Drinking Matters*: *Public Houses and Social Exchange in Early Modern Central Europe*. He has described church houses as 'prime examples of interactions between the sacred and the profane in late medieval communities. As facilities for stone-masons embellishing ecclesiastical buildings or worshippers in need of physical restoration, church houses supported the religious life of their parishes – as socio-cultural centres and communal assets'. A forerunner of the working men's club, affiliated to the Church, of course!

Prior to the middle ages, the local church was invariably the largest building in any community and the focal point of village life. It was used not only for religious services and meetings, but also for social celebrations that raised additional funds for parish obligations, such as the maintenance of the highways and provision of fire-fighting equipment.

Before the Reformation, there were more than a hundred Saints Days in the church calendar, with celebrations involving much dancing and drinking. This led them to be called 'church ales'. At first, such events were held within the church, particularly at Whitsuntide and May Day, with revels that included sports, plays and Morris dancing. However, by the mid-15th century, churches began to be used for worship alone. 'Church houses' (the medieval equivalent of the church hall) were therefore built in the churchyards, purely for the purpose of holding 'ales'. It became common practice for the churchwardens to arrange a 'brewing'; collecting ingredients from parishioners and then serving the ale at an event, often held on Sundays. Indeed, almost every time funds were needed for the church, they appear to have filled the vats, brewed their ale, and invited the parishioners to drink and be merry. In the 16th century, these events were sometimes referred to as a 'drynkyn'). There were 'leet-ales' (held on 'leet' – the manorial court day), 'lamb-ales' (held at lamb-shearing); Whitsun-ales, clerk-ales, church-ales, and so on. Some say that the word 'bridal' derives from the 'bride-ale' served at the wedding feast.

In 1633, Bishop Pierce of Bath and Wells, said of church ales that 'many poor parishes have cast their bells, repaired their towers, beautified their churches, and raised stocks for the poor'. With the growth of Puritanism in the late 17th century, church ales attracted serious disapproval and were considered sinful. There was great concern about the 'disorder' accompanying church ales, bastards conceived after the festivities, and many other 'inconveniences'. Under Oliver Cromwell, these events were banned, and redundant church houses were put to other uses to benefit the parish. For example, they may have become a school or an alms-house, or they may have been rented to a former landlord who continued to brew and sell ales. By the beginning of the 18th century, England had become a moral quagmire, with the country becoming increasingly decadent. Drunkenness was rampant and gambling was so extensive that one commentator of the time described England as 'one vast casino'. Thomas Carlyle (an eminent historian and teacher during the Victorian era), described the country's condition as 'stomach well alive, soul extinct'. The reaction of English people to this Scotsman's comments were not recorded, however it is safe to say that no one would be so foolish as to make such comments today.

Problem drinking - There were frequent complaints from employers that hard drinking was corrupting morals and destroying health, and this was not just the prerogative of men. Drunkenness continued to be a matter of great concern, particularly given the number of public houses. This situation was at odds with the Church's attitude, which appeared to encourage drinking (through church ales) rather that discourage it. In the 19th century, hard drinking was still a problem despite appeals from groups such as the Church of England Temperance Society, The League of the Cross, the Salvation Army and the British Women's Temperance Association. Even today, drinking is highlighted as the root of many problems yet still the Church appears to endorse this activity as a way of socialising. This is demonstrated by the number of current church wine societies; For example the Communion Wine Club, The Church of the Holy Name Wine Club, and a wine society in Hampshire that meets at the Chapter Room at Church Cottage Rooms.

The parish register at St Benet Fink (City of London records the death, in 1673, of the churchwarden, Thomas Sharrow, who literally got into a right pickle when he fell into a beer vault in Paternoster Row and lay there undiscovered for eleven days. The register entry includes the admonition 'let all who read this take heed of drink'.

The London Beer Flood of 1814 - The idea of an unlimited free supply of beer sounds wonderful, but when one million pints are delivered all in one go, the idea seems less appealing! Following a poor managerial decision made at a brewery, regarding the integrity of the large iron bands around an enormous wooden barrel (22 feet high), a tsunami of beer cascaded into surrounding streets.[48] The Henry Meux Horseshoe Brewery in Tottenham Court Road was situated among the densely populated, wretched houses and tenements of St Giles Rookeries (given its name because of the number of people living there). This was a notorious slum inhabited for many years by the poor, the destitute, prostitutes and criminals. They lived in squalor in basement rooms, without any sanitation whatsoever. A reformer once opined that it should be swept away in the interest of health and cleanliness. It was here on 17 October 1814 that over 135,000 gallons of beer erupted. This caused nearby vats to do the same, creating a domino effect that resulted in a total of around 323,000 imperial gallons of beer filling the surrounding streets in a 15-foot high wave. Basements were quickly filled with the local porter beer. Despite the ensuing chaos, human nature soon kicked in, with people collecting the brown porter ale in any container that came to hand! Incredibly, only eight people were known to have drowned in the flood or died from their injuries. The stench of beer in the area persisted for months afterwards, perhaps improving the miasma that persisted before the incident!

A fund was set up by the churchwardens of St Giles and of St George's, Bloomsbury, for the relief of those affected. Within a month, more than £800 had been raised, including donations from two other breweries. As St Giles was the last church on the route from Newgate Prison to the gallows at Tyburn, the Churchwardens paid for the condemned to have a drink (popularly named 'St Giles' Bowl') at the pub next door, the Angel, before they went to be hanged. A further demonstration of the churchwardens' generosity.

Ecclesiastical pubs - Whilst I have come across many pubs with ecclesiastical names, particularly 'Church House', I have found only one celebrating churchwardens. Well, in this case, twenty churchwardens. Cockley Cley near Swaffham in Norfolk has a pub called the Twenty Churchwardens, a name originating from the annual meeting of clergy and churchwardens of the Deanery of Cranwich, which used to gather there. Snippets of history from newspapers and personal reflections might suggest that the 200-year-old building started life as a 'church house', passing through various uses, serving as the village hall and school before finally returning full circle to its original purpose.

Theatrical entertainment - Like many Puritans, William Prynne[49] (a 17th-century English lawyer) abhorred decadent celebrations such as religious feast days and various forms of entertainment such as stage plays. Prynne was not short of words when writing his ponderous book *Histriomastix*. In this anti-theatrical diatribe, he savagely ridicules the immorality of acting, dancing, and other such pursuits. On the sin of dramatic performance, he says, 'but now-a-dayes Musicke is growne to such and so great licentious-nesse, that even at the ministration of the holy Sacrament all kinde of wanton and lewde trifling Songs, with piping of Organs, have their place and course. As for the Divine Service and Common prayer...' He goes on to attack the English Renaissance theatre and celebrations such as Christmas, noting 'our Christmas lords of misrule, together with dancing, masks, mummeries, state players, and such other Christmas disorders, now in use with Christians, were derived from these Roman Saturnalia and Bacchanalian festivals, which should cause all pious Christians eternally to abominate them'. This tome of over 1,000 pages condemns most aspects of dramatic performance popular during the era, from the practice of boy actors representing women, to the 'obscene lascivious love songs, most melodiously chanted out upon the stage'. Prynne was severely punished by the Court of the Star Chamber at Westminster Palace for writing this book. He was fined £5,000 and sentenced to be pilloried twice, mutilated by the severance of his ears, and imprisoned for life. In addition, he was expelled from his university and prohibited from practising law. Minus ears, he was released from prison and elected to the House of Commons in 1648!

Four hundred years ago, churches in England were sometimes used as 'playhouses' for travelling actors, just as they occasionally serve as theatres for plays and concerts today. Most performances were local, amateur productions. However, provincial church buildings were sometimes made available as temporary playhouses for professional touring companies, too. Travelling troupes also played in the private homes of leading burgesses and in the country houses of local gentry, as they needed to maintain the patronage of a noble household to promote their craft. They performed their plays in guildhalls (which they rented for the occasion) as well as in schoolhouses, churches and church houses.

During this time, churchwardens would need to be on their mettle, as travelling actors were perceived as a threat. The prevailing legal system in England defined actors who travelled about the country as 'masterless men' and vagabonds, and treated them harshly. Despite this, they were free to perform any play, some of which may have contained content of a dubious nature, speaking against the State or expressing seditious or heretical ideals.

As women were not allowed to perform on the English stage, boy players in the age range of 8-12 years old were much sought-after to play female roles, as their voices were not 'broken'. Since the middle ages, companies of children had grown out of cathedral choirs and similar institutions. They were musically talented, strictly disciplined, educated in the trivium (grammar, logic, rhetoric), and were sometimes fluent in Latin. The boys were formidable competition for the companies of adult actors in Elizabethan England and they became known as Children of the Revels.

While controversial in their time, the children's companies had been effective in funnelling talented, educated, and experienced young actors into the adult companies. In these times, there were no safeguarding laws to protect the innocence of children. Young boys were snatched on their way to school by 'child catchers' who roamed the streets of London in the late 16th and early 17th centuries. They were then forced to perform on the stage, often in seedy theatres for the titillation of predominantly male audiences. Even Queen Elizabeth I was implicated in this practice, by signing warrants allowing theatre bosses to capture children for their companies.[50]

Many Puritan preachers, who hated the theatre in general, were outraged by the use of boy players. They believed that the practice encouraged 'unnatural behaviours' such as kissing and other gestures. Thomas Heywood, an actor-playwright of the time, protested that 'to see our youths attired in the habit of women, who knows not what their intents be? Who cannot distinguish them by their names, assuredly knowing they are but to represent such a lady, at such a time appointed?'

In 1604, Church Canon Law No. 88 stipulated that churches were 'not to be profaned'. Churchwardens or quest-men and their assistants were directed to suffer no plays, feasts, banquets, suppers, church ales, drinking sessions, temporal courts, leets, lay-juries, musters, or any other profane usage of the church, chapel or churchyard.

Chapter 13

RELIGIOUS DISSENTION AND RECUSANCY

Religious dissention began long before the Reformation. Indeed, in the 14th century, the Lollards, under the guidance of John Wycliffe, challenged conventional beliefs. Their actions had grown from dissatisfaction over corruption in the Catholic church. These people were sometimes called 'religious delinquents.' Wycliffe held the firm belief that the Pope was second in authority to the scriptures, to which Pope Gregory responded by calling him a 'master of errors'.[51] The Lollards were so named as they muttered and mumbled when reading texts (from the Dutch word *lollaerd*). However, by the mid-15th century, 'lollard' had generally come to mean 'heretic'.

English Catholics who remained loyal to the Pope were not tolerated after the Pope refused to accept Elizabeth I as Queen of England, considering her to be illegitimate. The subsequent 'Recusancy Acts' made attendance at an Anglican church compulsory and those who refused to do so were declared 'recusants'. The 'Test Acts' served as a religious scrutiny of those seeking public office, imposing various civil restrictions on both Catholics and non-conformists seeking such positions. As local administrators of the law, churchwardens had little choice other than to comply with royal diktat (despite their personal religious beliefs). To rebel would be considered an admission of recusancy, most probably resulting in imprisonment. The law was not always strictly enforced, especially in the smaller towns and villages where communities were close-knit. Churchwardens might have chosen to take a softer approach when dealing with recusant friends and relatives, to avoid actions that might have had them excommunicated and barred from attending *all* church services and from burial in the graveyard. Rather than displease neighbours, relatives or others in higher authority, churchwardens may have preferred to risk perjury and employ 'promoters' (informers) to do the reporting for them.

Jews were prevented from complete social integration (especially from various professions and Parliament) due to their inability to take the Christological Oath, or the sacrament that would confirm their loyalty to the established Church and State. By the 17th century, the Jewish communities began to be more socially and commercially diverse and they became involved members of their local communities, integrating into the class system. It was not until 1858 that the Christological Oath was amended in Parliament, leading some years later to complete equality for Jews and Christians. Integration brought mutual benefit, although Jews were still subjected to various oaths by both religious faiths. Talmudic Law prohibits the consideration of bribes in any negotiation, even if both parties believe it to be of mutual benefit or acting in the public interest. In the following cases, a degree of chicanery might have been employed to avoid suspicions of bribery.

In 1775, the Registry of the Prerogative Court of Canterbury detailed the will of one David Franco (a millionaire philanthropist) and his generous gifts, including multiple donations to local Christian churches and hospitals. These donations were to be managed jointly by the *gabbai tzedakah* (the Jewish community collector) and the churchwardens and overseers of the Christian churches. It is also interesting to note from Palgrave's Dictionary of Anglo-Jewish History, that in 1850, Henry Keeling (born Levy) generously donated to repairs at St George's Church in Botolph Lane, Billingsgate. He later placated two belligerent congregations, after which he was unanimously elected churchwarden, the first practising Jew to do so.

The Jewish community bankrolled many small business enterprises during times when Christian usury was strictly controlled. Indeed, all Jewish financial dealings were administered by a discrete branch of the Exchequer – the Exchequer of the Jews.[52] In 1275, when Jews were forbidden to lend money they instead became landlords, providing around 9% of the total student accommodation at Oxford University. The Abbey at Bury St Edmunds, once one of the richest and most powerful Benedictine monasteries in England, became almost equally indebted by the sum of over £2,000, to both the Jewish community in Norwich and two local benefactors.

Chapter 14

THE RISE OF NON-CONFORMANCE

The National Archives describes non-conformists (dissenters) as those who did not belong to the Church of England. In 1675, Lord Treasurer Danby sought to convince Charles I of the popularity of the Church of England, so he instructed the Archbishops of Canterbury and York to undertake censuses to determine every parishioner's religious stance. With the assistance of the churchwardens, a survey was completed asking each parish three questions: (a) the number of inhabitants; (b) the number of Popish recusants or persons suspected of recusancy; and (c) the number of dissenters. As the wording of the census questions was ambiguous and varied from one ecclesiastical jurisdiction to another, it resulted in huge inconsistencies in recording accuracy.[53]

The recusancy laws were doomed to fail from the start due to difficulties in recovering fines. The cost of housing offenders in prison would, over time, result in a tacit acceptance of other faiths. Only Catholics, identified as blatant or persistent absentees from Anglican church services, would be referred to the courts where they would suffer various types of punishment such as fines, property confiscation, and ultimately imprisonment. The growth of hardcore recusancy was almost impossible to break. The Chester diocese had a substantial number of 'obstinate' recusants and despite strenuous efforts by the authorities, their resolve could not be broken, resulting in a significant number being imprisoned. In the 1580s, recusants were imprisoned at Chester Castle. However, this was the main port in the north-west that provided an easy escape route to the sea, so prisoners were moved to Manchester Recusant Prison. Later, all recusants, except persistent offenders or the rich, were released due to the cost of their upkeep.

There were far more pressing matters to be dealt with. The clergy were seen to be leading worldly lives; dressing richly and living in luxury. Confidence in the Church was waning, with a feeling that its power was being used for personal advantage rather than for the general good of the people. All this was confirmed by John Colet,[54] the Dean of St Paul's Cathedral in London, who was scathing in his comments regarding the state of the Church and the need for drastic change. He warned that 'priests should set an example for others as a beacon of light' and cited four evils that constitute the corruption of priestly living: devilish pride, carnal concupiscence, worldly covetousness and worldly occupations. He further reinforced this comment by stating that 'every corruption, all the ruin of the Church, all the scandals of the world come from the covetousness of priests.' Colet also believed that heretics (recusants) were not nearly so great a danger to the Protestant faith as the wicked, indolent lives of the clergy.

People wanted religion but were dissatisfied with its leaders and their teachings. They resented the monopoly of the Church and believed every priest had a right to preach what he chose. As a result, a movement for religious freedom spread, with many people in northern Europe founding new churches of their own. Their members became known as non-conformists. In 1846, Parliament passed the Religious Disabilities Act which removed the last restrictions against dissenters and Catholics. The Act also extended to Jews the same rights and freedoms on education, property and the administration of charities.

Chapter 15

PRESENTMENTS AND VISITATIONS

Every year, at the time of the annual parochial church meeting, the current churchwardens are required to complete the bishop's 'articles of enquiry' form, which not only gathers information on the running of the parish church but also gives the PCC an opportunity to share information about life in their church. These forms are sent to the archdeacon and they become part of the visitation process.

This type of process has been in existence for many hundreds of years. In the past, presentments (as they were known) were based on the replies received to the articles of enquiry that the bishop sent out as the basis for his visitation. The process sought to ensure that parish churches were in good repair and had the required fittings, furnishings and religious artefacts. Each church was required to report on the condition of the fabric and its curtilage, church attendance numbers, problems with non-conformists and the morals of the parishioners. This included all blasphemers, swearers, drunkards, and usurers. Even the performance of the clergy had to be commented on!

Churchwardens have always been admitted by the bishops and they are their representatives in the parishes. This tripartite relationship of bishop, churchwardens and incumbent has not always been an easy one. Each has had their own agenda and personal goals, which has sometimes obscured the fulfilment of the three theological virtues of faith, hope and charity. During the 15th century, political and religious tensions increased. Discontent among the laity regarding the behaviour of the clergy at all levels sometimes resulted in cases of assault on clergymen.

Thomas Gascoigne, the Chancellor of Oxford University and respected theologian, was outspoken in his *Liber Veritatum*, in which he highlighted the year 1450 as significant for assaults on unpopular bishops, two of whom were killed by mobs. Many people objected to the unseemly behaviour of the bishops who were seen as rich, indulgent and negligent of their preaching. They partook in human pleasures whilst at the same time expecting religious observance and subservience from the laity. Gascoigne reinforced these views in his sermon entitled 'The Seven Streams of Babylon', in which he highlighted the many lazy and lurid evils of the clergy in general.

It would seem that bishops have always reserved their right to unpopularity. In his departing speech in 2012, the Archbishop of Canterbury, Dr Rowan Williams, said 'risking unpopularity, taking the flak, is what archbishops are here for – it is the stuff of the job'. He went on to say 'it is something you realise the more you work here, that maybe Britain benefits from having someone to get angry with, and that compared to my predecessors I have got off lightly'. (*C'est la vie.*)

Prior to the Reformation and even into the early reign of Henry VIII, parishioners must have lived in relative harmony with each other. However, when Henry made the decision to break from the Catholic faith and make himself head of the English church, he triggered the start of a challenging period lasting many centuries, during which people had to make decisions about their faith that impacted their lives, possibly resulting in persecution or worse.

The 16th and 17th centuries were extraordinary times for all religious administrators. There were regular and tempestuous changes in doctrine and doxology, coupled with socio-religious manoeuvring that challenged accepted beliefs. During this time, the clergy and churchwardens would have been caught between their bishop's agenda for reform and their own unwillingness to betray friends and family by divulging sensitive information that could harm relationships and bring about retribution. Over the centuries, the mutual dislike and mistrust between the clergy and the bishops has been well documented. The example of a bad lifestyle set by the bishops was exacerbated by the view they had of themselves as being wise and shrewd. They were perhaps intelligent but lacked common sense; what someone once described as 'clever sillies'. This was reciprocated by the bishops' expressions of discontent with the clergy. This was strange as well as naive, inasmuch that it was the bishops who would have appointed the clergy and also approved the churchwardens. In defence of the clergy at a parochial level, the upheavals of the Reformation had resulted in the loss of half their number. Of the remainder, only half had been educated at university, the rest coming from local grammar schools.

As I have said earlier, the churchwardens had to act with guile and profundity in order to maintain good relations with clergy and parishioners (and ultimately the bishop). No more so than when presentments were made to the bishop. Annually, the bishops delivered a charge to the diocese, a sort of 'state of the nation address' that was made after the completion of his visitations.

Bishop William Lloyd of Peterborough undertook his personal parish visitations in 1680, with few illusions about the efficiency of the traditional visitation procedure. In a letter to William Sancroft (the Archbishop of Canterbury), he wrote 'the defects can never be known by the presentments of the Churchwardens [who] will forswear themselves over and over rather than bring expense on themselves and on their neighbours'.[55] The expectation was that presentments would be handwritten, although parish administrators were devious and often supplied them with pre-prepared (or printed) forms that only required signatures to be added. Some merely stated *omnia bene* (all is well). Over the years, the volunteered information became less detailed and some returns showed clear signs of collusion in their compilation. Some, signed by the churchwardens, were obviously composed by the minister who had even had the arrogance to complete the section entitled 'concerning the minister'.

The visitation process was seen as central to the rebuilding of trust, however the unwillingness of churchwardens to participate and to identify neighbours for ecclesiastical and moral offences demanded a fresh approach[59]. From the late 17th century, some bishops sought to involve the clergy rather than the churchwardens in the process and to make visitations a more administrative occasion than a judicial one. New questions were addressed directly to the parochial clergy, seeking details of population, pastoral provision, educational initiatives and charitable provision, and in some cases, the social and political complexion of their parishes. Some bishops entered the information provided by the parish clergy into a survey, or *speculum*, for their own use and for their successors. Bishops used the opportunity to ensure that the clergy were discharging their responsibilities and to remind them of the role of the Church in both religious and social matters. Subsequently, a citation was issued to all churches, along with a book of articles in which the churchwardens were to make their presentments, covering issues such as non-attendance, offences against moral law, and administrative matters.

The situation had not improved by the 18th century and a number of bishops continued to express dissatisfaction with the way in which churchwardens were replying to the visitation articles that they had been sent, requesting information from the parishes. In 1742, Bishop Nicholas Clagett decided to issue a rebuke to his clergy, which the churchwardens should have treated with suspicion and ambivalence as the letter addressed them as 'Good Brother'. It continued 'in order to obtain a proper knowledge of the present state of my Diocese which, I am sensible, I cannot have without the Assistance of my Reverend Brethren... You will oblige me by sending as full and particular answers as you can... And because it is possible that some man's answer in this matter may be construed as an Accusation of himself, I promise that no such answer shall be used as evidence against any Person subscribing'.[56]

The enthusiasm of the bishops did not go unnoticed by the newspapers of the time. In September 1834, an article appeared in the Sunday newspaper *Bell's New Weekly Messenger*, which was in response to the Bishop of London's charge (his address to the synod). The journalist informs us that the bishop's charges were seldom remarkable and that this one (after an absence of four years) was no exception. He begs the question: when will the bishops be wise? The following is a précis but you will get the gist... 'Like Angels' visits, they are few and far between. The bishop is innoxious (useless) except in the House of Lords and should be left to enjoy his enormous unearned revenue. Leave him alone and he will even live for 20 years, in Italy, like the bishop of Derry. He is a thorough-paced aristocrat whose doctrine is that all evils must fall on the poor and advises that clergy wages should be enhanced from tax revenues – to put them out of the temptations of subservience'.

Bishop William Lloyd of Peterborough conducted a personal parochial visitation of his relatively compact diocese. He saw personal supervision as invaluable in bringing the inferior clergy and churchwardens to 'a serious sense of their duty', but few of his contemporaries were as assiduous as he in this matter. Bishop Thomas Secker (the Archbishop of Canterbury) appeared to be altruistic, seeing the enquiry questionnaires as an opportunity to involve the parish clergy more directly in the visitation process and as a vehicle for discussion of church affairs at all levels, from the parochial to the national. The clergy could be assured that their lives and opinions would be closely scrutinised, not just in matters of church law but also in politics. This situation could be viewed as ironic. The bishops were recovering the power they had enjoyed in centuries past when they nominated parish priests from the ranks of monks at the monastery, which consequently had caused them to be mistrusted as the parishes thought they had their own agenda.[57]

More recently, the Dean of Peterborough, the Very Revd Charles Taylor, resigned with a stinging attack on envious people at the centre of the Church of England who resent 'uppity' cathedrals and who wish to impose a 'monochrome blandness' on the Church.

The Dean dropped a strong hint that his decision to leave had been forced upon him, with some people alleging that the manner in which it was effected was legally dubious, morally reprehensible, and pastorally disgraceful. He replied, in the manner of Francis Urquhart in the Michael Dobbs 1990s political drama 'House of Cards', "You might very well think that; I could not possibly comment." [58]

Today, the archdeacon's parochial visitation happens every three years. During the visitation, the bishop, or more likely the archdeacon, pays a visit to each parish church. As officers of the bishop, churchwardens have to report regularly on the state of affairs at the parish church and report anything that may be amiss. Churchwardens must respond to all questions posed by bishop or archdeacon regarding church property, and report any irregularity or failure in duty of which the incumbent is guilty. The archdeacon must inspect all parochial registers and records held in the parish: the terrier and inventory (Canon F17), the logbook (Canon F13(4), the minute and account books, insurance policies, the PCC's policies on child protection, employees' contracts, and insurance policies. They must review progress on quinquennial works and inspect the storage of valuables, the buildings and curtilage, and the security and safety systems. They must also see the PCC's mission action plan. Each visit generates a report that will be sent to the parish.

A Church of England report in 2008 entitled 'Quality and Quantity Issues in Ministry' suggested that the standard of new clergy had deteriorated due to eagerness to fill vacant posts and many long-standing vicars losing their energy and enthusiasm. The majority of bishops believed that most new candidates did not have the necessary skills and abilities. The report described contemporary worship as feeble and sweet, leading no one to the Majesty of God.

As part of the drive to improve priestly performance, the Church would encourage its clergy to consider how they could deliver better sermons. A new book entitled *Preaching with Humanity: A Practical Guide for Today's Church (2008)* advised congregations to offer their vicar constructive criticism rather than the well-intentioned pleasantries normally exchanged at the end of a service. It even (radically) suggested that clergy should urge their parishioners to post blogs giving their opinion on the sermons and plans for the church!

Today, we are too polite to make challenges from the congregation. Or are we? In 2016, a Church of Scotland minister began to encourage his congregation to challenge his sermons in real time via text. He believes that, rather than being a hindrance during services, mobile phones can help the congregation to be engaged and so to grow and flourish. Brave man!

Chapter 16

ENVIRONMENTAL MANAGEMENT

Wildlife Warden (I think not) - The Preservation of Grain Act of the mid-16th century made it compulsory for every man, woman and child to kill as many animals as possible that appeared on an official list of 'vermin'. The Act was created to counter food shortages caused by the spread of disease by animals, that had resulted in a series of bad harvests. Churchwardens were instructed to pay people for physical evidence of having killed creatures, some of which were harmless. The payments ranged from a penny for the head of a kite or a raven, to 12 pence for a badger or a fox. These were large sums when the average agricultural wage was around 4 pence a day. Some people believe that the demise of animals such as the hedgehog, wildcat and many other creatures is due to the mass slaughter during this time. Churchwardens' records from the 17th and 18th centuries highlight a dispassionate dichotomy when comparing the money given for the capture of vermin (4 pence for each head of a hedgehog) and the 2 pence compensation given to a serviceman maimed during battle. Foxes would later be exempted when the gentry commenced their 'sport' of fox hunting!

The Environmental Warden? - In 2007, *The Argus*, a Brighton-based newspaper, published the headline 'Vicars urged to cut down on holy water use'.

Environmentalists were claiming that faith groups were using too much water and they were being urged by religious leaders of all faiths to go green. Perhaps an over-dramatic statement, although it did raise awareness of the emergence of Ecofaith, a multi-faith partnership promoting ways of sustainable worship. As to whether it is safe to recycle holy water poses an ecclesiastical conundrum. St Teresa's Church in Dublin had an outside tap dispensing 'take-home holy water' and there are many open sources of holy water throughout the world. However, the advice given by microbiologists is to be wary regarding the source of holy water. Perhaps we should heed the old joke: 'How do you make holy water?' 'You boil the hell out of it!'

The aim of 'Shrinking the Footprint', the Church of England's national environmental campaign, is to make significant improvements in ecological management from parishes through to palaces. The Environmental Policy Officer for the Church of England is hoping that the creation of environmental champions in each parish will lead to better churchyard management by promoting a haven for wildlife and plants. Vicars and churchwardens will be asked to draw up plans for the more modern use of churchyards. For example, yew trees, essential for the making of longbows, used to be grown in churchyards because they were banned from open pasture, as their berries poisoned livestock. What new species could be planted to meet modern needs?

God said 'let there be light', however, with the environmental guidance manual 'Don't Stop at the Lights', churches are being encouraged to ration it, saving energy in the process. They are especially encouraged to only use floodlights for special occasions. Written by the authors of How Many Lightbulbs Does it Take to Change a Christian? (David Shreeve and Claire Foster-Gilbert) the book promotes initiatives for leading churches through a changing climate.

The Church of England has led by example to reduce the carbon footprint of the country. An ambitious target has been set to reduce carbon emissions by 80%, by the year 2050. In 2016, Gloucester Cathedral set the benchmark for other churches by becoming the first cathedral in the world to be fitted with an array of solar panels.

Chapter 17

WITCHCRAFT AND MAGIC

During the medieval period and beyond, there were alleged cunning folk and wizards in every village. They were known by a variety of names depending on their particular brand. There were nigromancers, necromancers (summoning spirits), seers, blessers, dreamers, soothsayers, enchanters, fortune-tellers and even girdle-measurers, who claimed to be able to tell whether fairy spells had been cast by measuring a person's waist! Churchwardens sought constantly to suppress or eradicate them.

Witchcraft in the middle ages was feared throughout Europe and the two most 'popular' types of magic were practised during these times. These were 'black magic' (nigromancy), which was associated with the devil or satanic worship, and 'white magic' (natural magic), a 'good type' associated with betterment and healing. In these times, people feared witches. They were superstitious and used charms as a means of defence. Magic was a 'cottage industry' in England for centuries. People who practised white magic were known as 'wise men' or 'cunning women' (don't ask me why) and their job was to help people.

The private use of magic was not just confined to the ignorant laity. According to local historian F.W. Hackwood, churchwardens in Wolverhampton consulted a 'wise man' when the church was robbed in 1529. The *Black Country Bugle* newspaper reported in 1614 that a local wise man (a recovery agent) was infamous for his dealings in the Black Country. Apparently, he would use a crystal ball to convince his customers that he could see exactly where stolen goods were located! Similarly, in 1583, the churchwardens in Thatcham, Berkshire, used a 'cunning woman' to identify who had stolen Communion table cloths. There are many similar records of churchwardens using 'alternative' practices to recover stolen goods. Very often, these 'wise' men and women were in partnership with local villains, running a very lucrative racket between themselves.[59]

People accused of witchcraft were persecuted throughout the medieval period and punishments were severe (and obscure). A common method for proving that someone was a witch was 'swimming' or 'ducking', in which the accused was tied hand and foot and immersed in the village pond. If the accused floated, it was considered that the water (God's creation) had rejected them and they were deemed guilty. However, if they sank (and drowned), they were innocent! Other less terminal tortures were also used to elicit confessions by using thumbscrews, whipping, stocks, etc. Ultimately, people were burnt at the stake, although this was less common than hanging, pressing or drowning. All such punishments fell into disfavour and had virtually disappeared by the late 18th century. St Augustine took a more empathetic approach, saying if a pagan believed in magic it was his 'error to believe in some other divine power than the one God'.[60] In his view, the church had no reason to seek out and punish witches because their powers did not exist.

The accusation of witchcraft was controversial, and often the simple act of 12 people attesting the accused's innocence resulted in the charge being dropped and a fine imposed in place of more severe punishment. Within the diocese of York, in the late 16th century, around half of the sorcery cases were dismissed without any action being taken.

Chapter 18

'PECULIERS'

The concept of the 'peculier' is a complex one dating from Anglo-Saxon times, when a church could ally itself with the monarch and consequently become independent from the bishop. Most peculiers survived the Reformation. With the exception of royal peculiers, they were finally abolished during the 19th century by various Acts of Parliament, becoming subject to the jurisdiction of a geographic diocese. A few non-royal peculiers still exist, but the majority of royal peculiers remaining are situated within the diocese of London. There is evidence to suggest that in the 16th century, churchwardens (appointed by ecclesiastical courts) visited peculiers to gather evidence for their 'presentations', detailing the behaviour of the parishioners and the state of the fabric of buildings and artefacts. Perhaps these were the original breed of 'peculiar' churchwardens! The situation regarding peculiers may now be subject to general review following a series of disputes at Westminster Abbey. An independent report drawn up by senior churchmen and lawyers, and published by the Lord Chancellor, found faults in the way that the Abbey was administered, citing that it was too secretive and unaccountable. Reforms in 2004 resulted in Queen Elizabeth II losing exclusive control over Westminster Abbey and other royal chapels.[61]

Rev. John Masding was the chairman of the English Clergy Association. In the summer of 2000, in an article in the Church Society publication *Cross†Way*, entitled 'Churchwardens: A Peculiar Breed', he discussed the unique position of churchwardens. However, John was far from ordinary himself and he may have been described as peculiar, in the nicest possible way. He was quintessentially British. He lived a rich and varied life and was often spotted driving in the streets of Birmingham in his vintage Bentley. He kept a well-stocked cellar and in retirement he was chairman of the Bath and County Club for some years (promoted to Bath's Premier Private Members' Club). I suspect that he also possessed a mischievous sense of humour, given that during a debate on the approaching imbalance of the sexes in the clergy, he described the situation as the 'Mothers' Unionisation of the Church'.

Archdeacon Thomas Colley, rector of Stockton from 1901-1912, was a splendid eccentric whose rectory was named 'The Radical' in his honour. He had a glass-topped coffin made, and during one Sunday evening service he startled his congregation by climbing into his coffin fully robed and had himself paraded around the church to demonstrate that he was not afraid of dying.

The coffin was kept in his study and those who attended confirmation classes had to sit on it.

Chapter 19
ELECTION OF CHURCHWARDENS AND THE PCC

THE ANNUAL PAROCHIAL CHURCH MEETING (APCM)

It is normal for the election of churchwardens and the APCM election of PCC members to be held consecutively, however they are legally separate. A statutory notice of each election must be displayed for a period of at least 14 days, inclusive of the two Sundays before the meeting.

THE ELECTION OF CHURCHWARDENS (THE VESTRY MEETING)

The selection and appointment of churchwardens has stood the test of time and recent debates by General Synod on the Churchwardens Measure 2001 have confirmed the situation regarding their election at the Annual Vestry Meeting. Such events may be attended by all residents of the parish whose names appear on the register of local government electors for that parish; clergy resident in the parish and people of any faith or none. The whole community has a right to vote in the election of churchwardens as they represent all parishioners, not just the congregation; a relic from the time when churchwardens had important secular functions in the parish.

"Item 4 – Election of Churchwardens. Michael insisted, not a regime change."

The person nominated churchwarden must meet the eligibility criteria detailed in the Churchwardens Measure 2001. If the incumbent feels that there might be 'serious difficulties' between themselves and a particular would-be churchwarden 'in the carrying out of their respective functions', they can rule that only one churchwarden be elected by the parishioners, the incumbent choosing the second. The choice however is limited to one of the other candidates who have been nominated at the parish meeting. Should the parish fail to elect any churchwardens, then the matter will be referred to the archdeacon or bishop to resolve. In exceptional circumstances, the bishop has the power to give permission for the appointment of someone who does not meet the specified requirements. In such circumstances he must robustly justify such an appointment, which would be reviewed after one year.

Churchwardens do not take up office until they are admitted by the bishop or their representative (more commonly the archdeacon). It is this action that allows them to take up the office, not their election by the parish. Whilst the churchwardens are the bishop's officers, the bishop has no discretion to refuse to admit a validly elected churchwarden, even if they doubt their fitness for office. As churchwardens are the bishop's officers, they also resign their office to the bishop.

The Annual Parochial Church Meeting (APCM)

This meeting is also open to all those who are resident in the parish whose names appear on the register of local government electors. This serves the purpose of giving transparency to the workings of the parish church. However, only those on the electoral roll of the parish church may vote during this meeting.

Churchwardens' Etiquette

In the case of Palmer v Tijou (1824), Sir John Nicholl observed that 'it is [the churchwarden's] duty to attend the church for the very purpose of preserving order... [but] if they are dissenters from the established church, and from motives of conscience cannot attend its worship, they are allowed by law to serve the office by sufficient deputy'.[62] Further, in the case of Adey v Theobald (1836), an exasperated ecclesiastical judge complained about the extraordinary anomaly of non-Anglicans officiating as churchwardens, commenting that 'there are various duties of the office of a Churchwarden, pointed at and enjoined by the Ecclesiastical law which this person [a non-Anglican Churchwarden] could not perform...for instance... the preserving of order during Divine Service'.[63]

In the past, there have been particular difficulties when non-Anglicans have been nominated as churchwarden, given that any parishioner might be nominated. Jews in the city of London were regularly elected as churchwardens and overseers and they paid the required fines for accepting the privilege. Quakers, however, posed a particular difficulty. The Quaker movement (the Religious Society of Friends) began in England during the 1650s when Oliver Cromwell governed the country and overthrew the established political and religious order. Quakers held what were radical beliefs at that time, and professed strongly the principle of egalitarianism, holding all men equal in the eyes of God. They were persecuted for idolatry – for not attending church and for holding meetings which were deemed to involve the false worship of God, under the pretence of preaching and teaching. They were also sanctioned for their refusal to swear oaths or to pay tithes, church rates and other dues; for conducting business affairs on first-days (Sundays) and holidays; for travelling on first-days; for being common nuisances and for contempt of court (for example, refusal to remove their hats); and for teaching without a bishop's licence. They caused churchwardens many problems.

On the issue of hat etiquette, to lift or doff the hat was once a universal sign of subservient regard, or at least of personal respect. With the Quakers' firm belief in the absolute equality of all men, they saw no reason to remove their hats even during a sermon, for it came from the lips of a man. However, when addressing God in prayer, they all arose and removed their hats. A high court case examined a certain Quaker gentleman who was accused of preaching without a licence. He was rebuked by the audience of bishops for keeping his hat firmly on his head and refusing to remove it, only doffing it momentarily during the hearing – to secular representatives. He was found guilty of refusing to observe the custom of 'hat honour' – removing one's headgear in the presence of a social superior. He was essentially indicating, in a silent yet provocative way, 'I reject your authority'. The political establishment took Quaker dissention very seriously. Their insistence on holding banned religious meetings in public led to 6,000 Quakers being imprisoned between 1662 and 1670.

Crockford's Clerical Directory gives direction on church etiquette, giving advice on how to address clerics at all levels of the hierarchy. However, it places the caveat that in offering its advice, it does 'not intend to imply that other practices are necessarily to be discouraged (for example, the use of Father as in "Father Smith"). A good deal depends on circumstances, and, where a personal preference is known, it is usually good practice to follow it'.[64] I take no radical stance on this matter, considering much of it to be 'horses for courses'. However, the use of the address 'Father' does raise issue, given the biblical passage in Matthew 23: 9 (NIV) which states 'and do not call anyone on earth "father", for you have one Father, and he is in heaven'. One local vicar with whom I came into regular contact would 'blank' you if you did not address him by prefixing his name with 'Father'.

THE CHURCHWARDEN AND THE BEADLE

The parish beadle was a minor official appointed by the vestry and subordinate to the churchwardens, overseers and constables. His job was multifarious and as obscure as the individual was pretentious, and no doubt very irritating. Often portrayed as corpulent, his flamboyant coat and cocked-hat were complemented by a large-headed staff (for show) in his left hand, and a small cane for *use* in his right. Pompously, he marshalled the children into their places and ensured that the churchwardens and overseers were duly seated in their allotted pews. The beadle was full of his own self-importance, and as Charles Dickens said in *Sketches by Boz*, 'the dignity of his office is never impaired by the absence of efforts on his part to maintain it'.

He kept order in the church during services, setting himself on a timber bracket provided for him at the head of the aisle, from where he scrutinised the congregation with his beady eyes, for any misdemeanours. He served as town crier, delivering news and dispersing noisy urchins. He patrolled the parish, resolved squabbles between parishioners and took drunks to the jail. A veritable jack of all trades and master of none.

Chapter 20

CHECKS AND BALANCES

Churchwardens assist the minister and even share the incumbent's cure of souls by providing bread and wine (not necessarily paying for it) and maintaining the correct balance between diocesan authority and parochial autonomy. That said, the churchwardens are not merely the incumbent's pastoral assistants. As Sir William Scott (registrar of the court of faculties and judge of the consistory court in 1788) highlighted, part of their office was to scrutinise the incumbent and any assistant clergy's performance of their official duties, by means of observation and complaint. He remarked that the balance was indeed a delicate one. It may be argued that this is partly undermined by the incumbent's chairmanship of the PCC and the ex officio membership of all other parish clergy. Sir William went on to say that the involvement of the clergy in PCC business is also open to objection, in that it leaves the clergy with less time for the ministry of the Word and Sacrament, which is their raison d'etre. Churchwardens must aim to facilitate the business of PCC meetings to ensure that all voices are heard and autocracy minimised.

Lord Hugh Cecil (Hugh Richard Heathcote Gascoyne-Cecil, 1st Baron Quickswood) was the eponymous leader of the 'Hughligans', a group of young privileged Tory Members of Parliament, critical of their own party's leadership. Lord Hugh always took a keen interest in ecclesiastical matters, and in a Church of England report 'Church and State' (1916), he voiced some outspoken views on parochial administration. These included a persuasive recommendation (never followed) that PCCs should be exclusively lay committees under the chairmanship of the churchwardens. However, this was not the view of the tactless incumbent of St Peter's Church, Roydon, Norfolk, who in 1969 stated his position clearly when he said 'my view is that the parochial church council does not represent the laity, but is part of my staff'.

I have some sympathy for Cecil's point of view, however I also appreciate the difficult and delicate relationship between incumbent and churchwardens. Whilst I was churchwarden, I regularly met with colleagues in the deanery. One colleague, when asked how things were at his church, would reply, 'Oh, you know, the same as ever. We attract new members and the vicar drives them out the door!' The relationship between incumbent and churchwarden should be collaborative, fostering mutual respect and diplomacy. As the diocese of Chichester reinforced recently in their advice on 'Being a Churchwarden', 'the relationship is of fellow-workers; not of a squire with his chaplain, nor of a mini-pope with his servants'.[65]

The relationship between incumbent and churchwardens, whether they are chosen by the incumbent or by the parishioners, was discussed by Sir William Scott in the case of Hutchins v Denziloe and Loveland (1792). The Rev. Hutchins prosecuted his churchwardens (Messrs Denziloe and Loveland) when they sought to obstruct and prohibit the singing of the choir accompanied by the organ during divine service. The churchwardens had acted that way because they supposed that, as they paid the organist and managed the choir, they (and not the incumbent) were to direct when the organ should or should not play. The reverend very obviously disliked his wardens, as he stated 'in the service Churchwardens have nothing to do but collect the alms at the offertory: and they may refuse the admission of strange preachers [visiting preachers] into the pulpit...but when advices of orders are produced, their authority ceases'.[66] Thus 'in all other respects, [the Churchwarden's] is an office of observation and complaint, but not one of control, with respect to divine worship'.[67]

The churchwardens' status as officers of the parish is of a lower profile than it used to be. Their common law duties towards the parish church and churchyard have been transferred to the PCC by the Parochial Church Councils (Powers) Measure 1956. However, the 1956 Measure did not alter the constitutional relationship between the churchwardens and the incumbent, nor the churchwardens' status as officers of the ordinary (the bishop). Canon E1(4) affirms that churchwardens are ex officio officers of the ordinary. As their officers, the churchwardens traditionally flank the bishop in procession when they attend their church.

Chapter 21

THE PUBLIC WORSHIP REGULATION ACT

The brainchild of Archibald Campbell Tait, the Archbishop of Canterbury, the Public Worship Regulation Act received royal assent in 1874. It was a particularly contentious issue which sometimes descended into violence, such was the strength of feeling toward it. A dark period in the history of the church.

The churchwardens have always been adept at managing 'red tape', and never more so than during the late 1800s when the Public Worship Regulation Act was being debated at all levels of society. The purpose of this soon-to-be notorious Act was to suppress the growth of pluralism and ritualism in the Church of England – or, as the Prime Minister, Benjamin Disraeli, put to the House of Commons, 'the mass in masquerade'. The problem was that the Church of England was being governed by obsolete laws that had been passed more than two hundred years previously, when Queen Elizabeth I sought a liberal theology as a compromise between the Church of England and the Roman Catholic Church. This theology was challenged by a group of Calvinist protestants called Puritans, who sought to reform the church by disposing of priestly robes and anything ornamental. They wanted a simpler kind of liturgy and the abolition of the episcopal system in favour of Presbyterianism. In this system, the church would be managed locally by a minister together with a group of elected elders of equal rank, and it would be governed by representative courts of ministers and elders.

The most controversial ritual practices, with Catholic origins, included the use of vestments, bells, incense, altar candles and unleavened bread. The orientation of the priest during the eucharist (facing east with their back to the congregation), making the sign of the cross, and mixing the wine with water, were also controversial. There were also other contentious practices relating to terminology, decoration and veneration. Churchwardens had to contend with the ambiguity of a process in which the views of *all people* (including non-conformists) living within the parish needed to be considered. Outraged Protestants responded with sermons, lawsuits, legislation and even mob violence in a long and futile campaign to halt the 'ritualist' movement. Under the Public Worship Regulation Act, churchwardens and aggrieved parishioners had the right to institute proceedings against the clergy for breaches of the law during the conduct of divine service. Sometimes, struggling to cope with the dissent of parishioners, they even resorted to locking the church to prevent the entry of clergymen nominated by certain bishops.

In order to promote unity between the various different sectors of the Anglican Church within the British Empire, a conference with all the Anglican bishops was convened in Lambeth in 1867, presided over by the Archbishop of Canterbury. By their third meeting, an agreement was reached that defined the basic tenets of the Anglican Church. It was a faith based on the Bible, with the Apostle's Creed and the Nicene Creed as the basis of belief. It acknowledged two sacraments – baptism and the eucharist – and an episcopal system. These conferences continue to convene every ten years to openly discuss topical subjects concerning the churches of the Anglican Communion (those in communion with the Archbishop of Canterbury).

Chapter 22

THE ORGAN SNATCHERS

Between 1540 and 1640, parishes suffered from dire problems that caused them distress, both economically and religiously. Bad harvests, disease and war put great strain on parish finances, resulting in the churchwardens being unable to provide relief to the poor. Many churches would have had to consider selling artefacts, including the organ, to raise money. The arrival of the Puritans with their stringent principles would have added further to the confusion. The Puritans (sometimes called 'precisionists' because of their strict codes of conduct) were morally enthusiastic Protestants who sought to purify the Church of England of Roman Catholic practices. They were strongly disapproving of music per se, and in church they were intent on the eradication of musical instruments and singing in services – or so they maintained. The arrival of the puritanical 'organ takers' was just another ball for the churchwardens to juggle. The removal of the organ would have been met with mixed emotions: devastation at the loss of a key element of church services, or perhaps it was a saving grace (no more repairs to pay for). Either way, they would have been coerced into allowing their prized possession to be made available to the highest bidder on the open market. Significantly, over 2,000 organs were destroyed when church interiors were cleansed of 'popery' by the Puritans and when Oliver Cromwell's Parliament issued an ordinance 'for the speedy demolishing of all organs'.

However, the Puritans did not always live up to their name. Whilst they sought to make bonfires from the 'recovered' artefacts, many of those items 'ironically' found ownership with the very people who sought to have them destroyed – the Puritans themselves. Indeed, Cromwell's love of music illustrated the contradictions of the Puritans.

The wholesale destruction or appropriation of organs must have been doubly aggrieving to William Prynne, an English lawyer, polemicist and author. He was a prominent Puritan, opposed to the church policies of the Archbishop of Canterbury. Not only were some of the misappropriated organs bought cheaply by tavern owners for musical evenings and 'music halls', others were acquired by Puritans for their own personal enjoyment. Indeed, Oliver Cromwell removed an organ from Magdalen Chapel, Oxford, and relocated it to Hampton Court where he employed a private organist for his entertainment!

Later, when organs were allowed in churches again, they were too expensive to be replaced. As a result, the great majority of church organs today date from the second half of the 19th century. Initially, choirs provided music (with no congregational singing). However, this music was not readily accepted by the social commentators of the time. Samuel Pepys and John Evelyn referred to it as secular music, suggesting that it was 'more appropriate to the taverns or playhouse rather than church!'

CHAPTER 23

FLARES AND GRACES (AND BLING)

Everyone had their own idea of the sort of vicar they wanted.

Churchwardens, I have found, tend to prefer a low profile, going about their business without drawing attention to themselves. Not so the clergy. Clerical decoration began in the 9th century, and in 1215 a church council made it mandatory for all Christian clergy to wear distinctive clothing, not necessarily as a status symbol, but to catch the public eye when out and about. Conversely, John Wesley, the founder of Methodism, was very clear on the subject of dress, stating that a Christian's apparel should be 'cheap, not expensive' and 'grave, not gay, airy, showy; not in the point of the fashion'. Everything in moderation.

Today, some might quote Exodus 28: 2-4 (New American Bible. Revised Edition) to support a case to retain their finery: 'For the glorious adornment of your brother Aaron you shall have sacred vestments made. Therefore, tell the various artisans whom I have endowed with skill to make vestments for Aaron to consecrate him as my priest. These are the vestments they shall make: a breast-piece, an ephod, a robe, a brocade tunic, a turban, and a sash'. Pope Francis would not agree, as he has called for a church geared to social justice, wanting church officials to live more modestly, suggesting that pastors must not be men with a 'princely mindset'. The American cardinal Raymond Burke must have missed this instruction as he was photographed in a lavish procession with a train of watered silk, fine scarlet gloves and a jewelled red hat. Also living profligately, the German bishop Franz-Peter Tebartz-van Elst spent €31 million renovating his official residence in Limburg!

High Anglicans have tended towards clothing that reflects the colours of the liturgical year, though often it is more flamboyant, pretentious and incongruent. Strange, as I cannot recall Jesus following Jacob's sartorial lead. Recently, the General Synod has debated this issue, exposing differing points of view. Some bishops prefer to adopt a humble dress code, whilst others hold the view that clergymen need to keep their 'episcopal bling' and the mitre should not be abandoned in an effort to look 'relevant' in 21st-century Britain. Abandoning these things would leave them feeling 'underdressed' in inner city areas of multicultural Britain.[68] A simple dress code did not hinder Mother Teresa, nor Ghandi, who declared that 'there is no beauty in the finest clothes if it makes hunger and unhappiness'. Mother Teresa's iconic blue and white striped sari was designed by her and copyrighted by her religious order to prevent imitation.

Sammy Johnson was a well-known Geordie actor who played 'Stick' in the BBC television series ' Spender' (also starring Jimmy Nail). Sadly, Sammy was killed in a freak accident in 1998 and subsequently the charity 'Sunday for Sammy' was set up in his name to benefit young performers. Sunday for Sammy is a series of biennial concerts aiming to embrace local artists, and in 2004 it featured a sketch entitled 'Bede's makeover'. A PR 'guru' is employed to boost the venerable Bede's boring appearance by recreating his persona, aiming to make him more media-friendly. After much debate, he is reborn as Josh Bede, the image enhancement completed with new 'threads' and a ' pad' on Newcastle quayside, replacing the decaying Jarrow Monastery. This forward thinking did not initiate innovative action by the Church of England 13 years later in 2017, when the General Synod granted permission for clergy to ditch their robes. It would no longer be 'Sunday best' and the robes have become 'surplice to requirements'. Clergy are now able to wear whatever they wish in an attempt to make the church more accessible and relevant to the modern world. Officially, they are able to lead services in casual clothing such as jeans and trainers, however one commentator said that this is not a charter for shell-suits, or jaffa cakes and coke. Another remarked that he enjoys dressing up in different clothes but he was concerned about losing his identity at themed weddings. The Archbishop of Canterbury was recently spotted wearing a pair of blue trainers, but he was adamant that they were 'walking shoes'. Methinks he doth protest too much!

Surplice to Requirements

The tabloid press are never slow to comment on Christian matters and the ordination of women bishops in the Anglican Church in 2014 was headlined with their usual 'subtlety'. The Oldie magazine (published by James Pembroke) carried a picture captioned 'Bishop's babes: Archbishop of Canterbury Justin Welby and women priests celebrating the 20th anniversary of female ordination', under a headline 'Vestments into frocks'.[69] *The Daily Telegraph,* however, went for a more colourful headline, with the unimaginative 'More teal vicar?'[70]

Vicars in Versace and bishops in Balmain. Research has shown that clergy are viewed by the general public as white-haired, middle-class men who wear dresses. However, each year, the Christian Resources Exhibition ('The Ideal Church Show') goes the full nine yards by hosting an event called 'Clergy on the Catwalk'. This cornucopia of Christian clerical couture supports some people's view that elaborate clerical garb has a particular appeal to clergy with a penchant towards being more flamboyant in their behaviour and who revel in it. *Vive la difference*! One vicar said, 'I have very little interest in church vestments [really?] but the CRE catwalk may become a road to Damascus. I have always wanted to be a model cleric but perhaps I will have to settle for being a clerical model.' (Mm.) Not to be left out, female clergy should no longer feel uncomfortable in clerical garb after the launch of a new female led enterprise. The website 'Collared clergy wear'[71] caters for the ladies with contemporary clothing for the modern clergywoman (Lace and Lycra; clergy clothing for curves.)

Years ago, Anglicans were opposed to non-conformists. How will this second coming be received? Thank goodness for the sensible, rational, circumspect (and modest) churchwardens, who prefer to dress soberly, achromatically in shades of grey, not wishing to upstage the bishop, nor clash with the stained-glass windows!

Chapter 24

NOTABLE CHURCHWARDENS

DEDICATION TO SERVICE

Commitment - In the 1990 s, a Staffordshire church was in need of ideas for its appeal to raise £136,000 for the restoration of the 170-year-old building. They settled on a bold and inspiring idea, that would also take them nearer to God. As it happened, it was April Fool's Day (a Sunday afternoon) when, guided by a steeplejack, that the churchwarden, an ex-churchwarden and the chairman of the appeal committee scaled the 100ft church tower. A local undertaker was spotted amongst the gathered crowd; a voice rang out in mordant humour - 'Pine with brass handles please'! Personally, I'd have settled on the idea of a parish ale to raise funds!

Long Service - Joe Scales, retired in 2010 after serving 50 unbroken years as churchwarden at two Teesside churches (31 years at St Thomas's Church, Glaisdale, near Whitby, and 19 years at St Hilda's, Liverton Mines, near Loftus. However, this is topped by Denis Buck of Grafton Flyford, who retired in 2015 after serving 55 years at the same church. He even remembers a boy chorister singing 'Hark the herald angels sing, Mrs Simpson's pinched our King!'

Never to be broken records.

The Famous

Edward VIII - When he was Prince of Wales, he became churchwarden of Sandringham chapel.

John Betjeman - An English poet, writer and broadcaster, who described himself in 'Who's Who' as a 'poet and hack'. He was Poet Laureate of the United Kingdom from 1972 until his death. He championed the social and aesthetic joys of Anglicanism in his many religious writings, such as *Poems in the Porch*. In 1937, he was appointed churchwarden at St. Mary's, Uffington, Oxfordshire.

Dorothy L Sayers - A renowned English crime writer, poet, playwright, essayist, translator, and Christian Humanist. Her father, the Rev. Henry Sayers, M.A., was a chaplain of Christ Church Oxford and headmaster of the choir school. Through her writings, she explored the stewardship of God's creation and the analogy of the trinity in the process of artistic creation.

Her churchwardenship was unusual in that there was no physical church. St Anne's in Soho had been bombed during the war and Dorothy served during the time when meetings were held in an adjacent building (St Anne's House). Dorothy's ashes are buried under the tower of St Anne's Church, Soho.

Enoch Powel - He had a surprise epiphany, given his early beliefs. Powell was heavily influenced by the German philosopher Friedrich Nietzsche. He initially adopted Nietzsche's concept that 'God is dead'. Despite his earlier atheism, Powell became a devout member of the Church of England, thinking in 1949 'that he heard the bells of St Peter's, Wolverhampton calling him' while walking to his flat. He subsequently became a churchwarden of St Margaret's, Westminster. Powell was a paradox who delicately bridged the dichotomy between racialist and racist, shown in his 'rivers of blood' speech in 1968.

THE INFAMOUS

As I said at the beginning of the book, Churchwardens might just as easily have been petty despots with their own aims and ambitions to fulfil, rather than sympathetic to the poor and needy of the parishes they served, as the following examples will demonstrate. Very obviously, these people bypassed the book of Proverbs and the wisdom and advice of Solomon.

Knobstick weddings - A knobstick wedding was the 19th-century equivalent of the shotgun wedding where, if an unmarried woman had a child and the father was known to the villagers, he would be chased around with a knobstick until he married her. A knobstick was a wooden club with a large knob on the end of it, used as a weapon, to coerce errant fathers. The whole point of this exercise was not necessarily to preserve virtue through marriage, rather it was a financial matter. Any woman who had a child out of wedlock was 'on the parish' – meaning that the community was responsible for housing them and finding them work (even if this was just in the workhouse).

After the passing of the Bastardy Act in 1733, churchwardens, overseers and constables had wide powers, and in cases of illegitimacy, where a child or expected child might become chargeable to the parish, considerable pressure was placed on the alleged father.

In cases of female paupers, parish officers would resort to bribery to absolve the parish of its burden of responsibility. They would marry off their female paupers by paying for the marriage licence, a gold ring, the church fees and a marriage feast, and they would also arrange a payment on completion of the marriage. These expenses would be charged to the parish which, of course, was illegal, but parish accounts in those days were sometimes carelessly kept and just as carelessly audited. There were also instances of more aggressive tactics being used to encourage marriage. The 6 October 1829 edition of *The Times* records that a man was coerced into marrying the woman he was accused of making pregnant. The authorities, referred to as the 'parish overseers', threatened to hang him if he did not go through with the arrangement. Feeling that he had no option, he agreed to the marriage and the pair were wed. However, those responsible for forcing the partnership were later called to face charges of 'fraudulently procuring the marriage'. As one 20th century comedian joked, 'for better, for worse, for richer, for poorer, but I did not think that it would be this bad!'

William Abbott - William was a shoemaker, churchwarden, and infamous highwayman, part of the notorious Culworth Gang who terrorised Northamptonshire for 20 years. He was the most flamboyant of the gang and always carried pistols on him, even when performing official duties in his church, St James The Less, Sulgrave, Northamptonshire. He cheekily stashed his loot in a chest in the church that can still be seen today. William was eventually caught and sentenced to death in 1787. Many of the gang were hanged, but William's sentence was transportation for life to Australia. He disappeared whilst awaiting deportation.

Joseph Merceron (The Boss of Bethnal Green) - St Matthew's, Bethnal Green is one of London's more noteworthy churches, having a colourful history with characters such as the exceedingly corrupt and scurrilous churchwarden Joseph Merceron,[72] the Kray family, and the radical priest Stewart Headlam (who helped to bail Oscar Wilde from prison at the time of his trials). The infamous Joseph Merceron became churchwarden in the early 19th century and lined his pockets from parish funds. He was jailed for 18 months in 1818 for stealing £1,000 from public funds (equivalent to over £80,000 in 2017). Strangely, he received a lenient sentence, and on his release from prison he resumed his old duties and continued to fleece the parish until his death in 1861. (*Friends in high places?*)

THE IGNOBLE AND IGNOMINIOUS

Churchwardens and the slave trade - Throughout history, there have been many people who have attempted to justify slavery, some doing so purely from a commercial self-interest, whilst others sought to show altruism. Aristotle, the great Greek philosopher, was one of the first to do so. He maintained that slavery was a natural thing and that there were two types of human beings – non-slaves and slaves. The first were born to rule and the second for subjugation. Souls of slaves were incomplete. They lacked the ability to think properly, so they needed to have masters to tell them what to do. St Augustine however, believed that the prime cause of slavery was sin. It was therefore inevitable and was appointed by God as a punishment for sin, beneficial to both slaves and masters. This would be later used by many as evidence of the acceptability of slavery.

King William III granted a charter to the Church of England's mission society, known as the Society for the Propagation of the Gospel to Foreign Parts (SPG), to spread the Gospel throughout British Colonies. Shortly after its formation, the society found itself the beneficiary of two sugar plantations in Barbados with some 300 enslaved Africans. This legacy was a gift from General Christopher Codrington, a former Governor-General of the Leeward Islands in the West Indies. His wish was that the 300 slaves 'would be kept and a number of scholars would be maintained there...taking care of the souls and bodies of the enslaved'.[73] He was so caring and concerned that he might lose the slaves that he boldly branded his 'sheep' with the word 'society', using a red-hot iron. An educational institution was built but the intention of slave education was never realised, and when the college opened in 1745, only white children were admitted.

The English had begun to colonise Virginia on the eastern seaboard of the USA, and also the British West Indies in the early 17th century. They introduced a system of civil, religious authority and parochial administration similar to that in England, however the laws relating to race and religion were quite severe. Parishes oversaw a wide range of responsibilities, including social welfare, with the churchwardens playing a key role in administering laws. There were significant extra responsibilities with respect to slaves, particularly with regard to inappropriate racial relationships and violations of the anti-miscegenation laws (interracial marriage and interracial sex), their consequences and their punishments. A number of bishops were entrepreneurial, or perhaps naively philanthropic, investing financially in crop plantations overseas, no doubt encouraged by the high financial gain and the promotion and validation of the practices by the SPG. Even if the churchwardens were bold enough to report the atrocious treatment of slaves (in their annual presentments to the bishops) they would, because of episcopal involvement, have fallen on deaf ears. One can only assume that churchwardens were complicit in slavery and the acts of deprivation and violence perpetrated on the slaves. Alternatively, perhaps out of fear, they turned a blind eye to events. Whichever the case, it is impossible to reconcile their actions with their sworn responsibility to maintain moral behaviour and pastoral support. Later, churchwardens would be authorised to sell slaves during the manumission (freeing) and they would rehabilitate them back into society. This activity may be cynically viewed as an attempt to either salve the conscience of the slave owner (investor), or to free the will of the individual slave; probably more the former than the latter.

More Recently...

Jimmy Saville - Deceased, disgraced and despised, he was made an honorary churchwarden at St John's Church, Cragg Vale in Calderdale, West Yorkshire, in recognition for the many thousands of pounds he had raised for the church. He helped during an interregnum and preached a sermon at the church, dressed in a lurid yellow and acid green hooded gown with a pom-pom brocade trim. He also presented the BBC programme 'Songs of Praise' from St John's.

"Give and it shall be given unto you"
(Luke 6: 38 -NIV)

As I said earlier in the book, churchwardens evolved into the treasurers of the Christian church and trusted guardians of its property. As members of the vestry, they became part of local democratic government. Today 'alternative' (often independent) churches do not subscribe to the ancient protocols of church management and with the rise of media promoted evangelism, this parish-centric management system and financial probity has been lost, leaving these churches open to abuses of authority.

Centuries before the term 'robber baron' entered the English vocabulary, the feudal system in England during the 11th century was sowing the seeds for future generations of colourful characters, such as ruthless sheriffs and power prelates who sought to increase their riches under the disguise of charitable giving. In 1642, Sir Thomas Browne (an English polymath) came up with the oft quoted phrase 'charity begins at home'. He said: 'But how shall we expect charity towards others, when we are uncharitable to ourselves? Charity begins at home, is the voice of the world; yet is every man his greatest enemy, and, as it were, his own executioner.' For centuries, people who should have known better have failed miserably to maintain their religious principles, misinterpreting that quoted phrase and promoting personal gain through blatant charity abuse.

During the 20th century, a new generation of latter-day John Wesleys began to appear, campaigning for the hearts and minds of evangelical Christians. Billy Graham was such a person. He gained much acclaim and respect, preaching to many millions during his global journeys. Billy began in the 1940s with a local radio show, and by 1950 he had gone national with his weekly radio broadcast called

'The Hour of Decision'. Billy had the foresight to register his organisation (the Blue Ridge Broadcasting Association) in 1950 to handle his affairs and ensure transparency.

All organisations need financial transparency to demonstrate their legitimacy, even more so televangelist churches or modern 'super' or 'mega' churches. Having virtual congregations devoid of the democratic process of parish councils, and guiding of the churchwarden's historic principles of financial and moral propriety, leaves these organisations open to the occasional rogue. There are many wacky autocratic entrepreneurial evangelists promoting their misguided brand of 'prosperity theology,' equating faith with material abundance. Promising their followers that God will reward their faith with tangible blessings for their faithful donations. During the 1980s, the prime promoters of this type of gospel were Jim and Tammy Faye Bakker, American Pentecostal televangelists. They initially used their 'Praise the Lord' Club (PTL) to promulgate their message engaging families through a (innocent) puppet show. Always pictured as immaculate and smiling, they presented a wholesome image, a 'squeaky' clean persona that attracted millions of followers to annually donate millions of dollars.

Adept at growing their audience, the Bakkers encouraged risk taking, extending people beyond their financial resources, counting on God to provide. Jim claimed that anyone could speak almost anything into existence, advising, 'Don't pray, "Lord, your will be done," when you are praying for health or wealth. You already know it is God's will for you to have those things.' 'If you want a new car, just claim it. Pray specifically; tell God what kind of car you want and be sure to specify what options.' (the l'Oréal epithet – 'because you're worth it'!) At its peak PTL grossed more than $100 million a year, funding the Bakkers lavish lifestyles. It is hard to believe, but the great evangelist Billy Graham was duped into endorsing them, something he would later regret when Jim Bakker was accused of infringing the majority of the ten commandments. Despite maintaining his innocence and blaming a satanic government conspiracy, Jim was sentenced, in 1989 to 45 years in prison for 23 counts of fraud and conspiracy. Convicted for illegally soliciting millions of dollars from his followers by selling them 'goods of dubious value'! His wife somehow escaped conviction and continued to defend their innocence and their hedonistic opulent life style.

After serving just five years in prison, Bakker was released. He allegedly sought humble forgiveness from the family of God he had offended, by hurt or shame, with his sinful and arrogant life style. Whilst he has disavowed the prosperity gospel, today he still hosts his own TV show, described by some as a 'Christianised version of QVC'. When in prison he must have a least read as far as the book of Revelation as he now advises on and sells products to prepare people for the arrival of the Apocalypse.

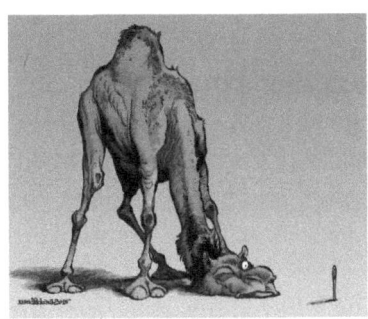

"Again, I tell you, it is easier for a camel to go through the eye of a needle than for someone who is rich to enter the kingdom of God." - Jesus.

Here in Britain, we are not immune from dubious pastors who prey on the vulnerable. They pedal medieval doctrines such as 'God wants you to give all your money to him and if you fail to pay your tithe, you do not really trust God'. They suggest that their tithe is an insurance against Satan , and warn them of the dire consequences of non-payment . Today , two of the fastest expanding and controversial churches in Britain have congregations of many thousands with annual tithed incomes of millions of pounds. Both registered charities , have fallen foul of the Charities Commission and have been investigated for financial irregularities . One has already been closed down and the other has been further investigated over lack of transparency relating to capital expenditure and extravagant personal property portfolios . Some of these churches have apologised to their congregations , not for the scale of their luxurious lifestyles but for the ' uncomfortable conversations' resulting from media headlines and public criticism.

Chapter 25

CHURCHWARDENS TODAY

A visitor to St. Leonard's Church, Warmingham recalls seeing a yellowing piece of paper. The passionate words recorded may have come from a churchwarden past. "We the willing led by the unknowing are doing the impossible for the ungrateful. We have done so much with so little for so long that we are now qualified to do anything with nothing."

Thankfully, times have changed and today's churchwardens, despite their perceived burdens, generally have a far easier life than their predecessors, given their lightened workload and support from the PCC. Gone are the political challenges of early 1800s when attempts were being made to commandeer parish expenditure, wresting it away from the controlling vestry and the churchwardens who had become chief executives of the parish.

But who should be churchwardens? - A debate in the House of Commons on the Churchwardens Measure 2001 advised that 'churchwardens are not only a bishop's appointees, but the people's choice. It is a very unusual position; they have two masters ... the people and the bishop'. Vicars should welcome constructive ideas and advice. But there needs to be a measure of mutual understanding and solidarity between incumbent and churchwardens.

The relationship is of fellow-workers; not of a squire with his chaplain, nor of a mini-pope with his servants! (Remember Rev. Hutchins court case.)

At times, things can go wrong and relationships and trust between an incumbent and the churchwardens break down, as has been demonstrated in recent years. The choice of incumbent is based on a statement of conditions, needs and traditions supplied by the PCC. From public records, it would appear that, despite this, the churchwardens in one southern UK diocese were initially unhappy with the suggested incumbent. However, perhaps under duress, they accepted the proposal. Over a long period of time, the actions of the incumbent, both his style and personality, caused concern to the churchwardens, such that they considered them to be detrimental to the life of the church. This acrimonious atmosphere eventually caused the churchwardens to submit a formal complaint against the incumbent, under the 2003 Clergy Discipline Measure. Despite the intervention of the bishop, his 'trouble shooters' and the appointment of a professional conciliator, all failed to bring about peace and harmony. Reconciliation between the churchwardens and the rector proved impossible. The result was the acrimonious resignation of the four churchwardens, who in their resignation said: 'We now believe that the rector is probably incapable of overcoming the difficulties he obviously has in many of his personal relationships. By stepping aside as your churchwardens at this time we hope that we may thus remove one of his problems.'[74]

The bishop's reply was equally conciliatory, saying that 'the churchwardens have been entirely proper in their concerns for the life of the parish all the way through and have wanted the best. It has just been one of those very unfortunate situations where a working relationship has not worked.' Although the incumbent returned to his parish, he 'retired' shortly afterwards.

Today's churchwardens inhabit a world of faculties, risk assessments, quinquennial reports and property maintenance (along with the associated jargon), as well as organising intercessions, rotas and religious service requirements. Whilst churchwardens have responsibilities, we must appreciate, and they must be reminded, that having responsibilities does not mean that they must personally carry out every specific function or duty. Rather, they must learn to delegate in order to ensure that 'stuff happens'. One could list the many attributes required to be a good churchwarden: faith, good listening skills, patience, organisation, understanding, empathy, tolerance, plenty of spare time… Oh, and every churchwarden's survival kit should include a sense of humour.

Nowadays, most churches employ the use of wireless microphones and whilst they are an invaluable tool, churchwardens (and the sound engineer) must be vigilant in ensuring that they are muted as the clergy move to the front door to speak to the departing congregation. It can be extremely embarrassing when personal conversations are broadcast to those remaining inside. Vicars come with a variety of personalities and are not immune to situations arising from their personal traits. An example of this is an insensitive remark (allegedly made by a parishioner standing close-by), regarding the vicar's tardiness towards work, which was picked up by the Reverend Slack's sensitive microphone. Oops.

During my time as churchwarden, I came to realise that having humility and being thick-skinned were also admirable attributes. Working as a business compliance manager with British Telecom, I well remember a delicate situation I once experienced whilst giving feedback to a team of managers on the results of a not-so-successful audit. I did not expect praise or even respect from the team, so I was very surprised when one manager spoke up by saying, 'Aye, I really admire Eric…' I just knew that a 'but' was going to follow. A deafening silence descended in the room as he continued, by doubting my parenthood. 'Aye, he was a… when I met him and he still is today.' My thoughts returned to a churchwardens' training event and the advice that we were given, which was, 'Don't take criticism personally. You can expect people to resist change and seek to personalise their anxiety.' Keeping going, I broke the silence by smiling, thanking him and reinforcing my position by saying that I always tried to be consistent. For the moment, the situation was defused.

Laterally thinking churchwardens - George Reynolds was both famous and infamous in the Darlington area. The millionaire owner of DirectWorktops and Darlington Football Club had, in his former life, been an enthusiastic safe breaker and entrepreneur who had spent time at her majesty's pleasure. He would shrug off his nefarious habits by saying that, 'God gives every one of us a gift...that's mine.' Despite this, he was a 'likeable rogue' or a 'fond fool', as north-easterners would say. George's reputation preceded him but he always maintained that he was a good man. One Sunday, just before the service, the churchwardens at Shildon Parish Church realised that the key to the safe had gone missing. 'Give George a call,' someone joked. No sooner said than done, George had been summoned (no pun intended) to church. He knelt before the safe, nimbly spinning the dial when a voice called out from behind. 'You ok George, or do you want the lights out?' 'The safe purred like a kitten,' George replied. 'I didn't even have to try the door – I heard the tumblers trickle.'

Chapter 26

THE TIMES THEY ARE A CHANGIN'

We are all aware that the digital age has arrived, however what is perhaps uncomfortable for the older generation is to see today's seamless morphing of 'trendy' vicars into 'techy' vicars' who embrace technology in all elements of the service. A reporter was interviewing a churchwarden who was retiring after 40 years of service to the church and asked:' You must have seen a lot of changes in that time?' " Aye," he replied, 'and I've resisted every single one of them.'

Frank Wappat was once described as a 'legend' at the local BBC in Newcastle upon Tyne. Before becoming a radio presenter (first with Radio 390, a pirate station), he was a ballroom promoter and an accomplished musician and singer. He worked in a 'western swing band' and other genres, yet he still found time to acquire a psychology degree. As a Methodist lay preacher, he soon got into trouble with the church who, he maintained, did not like his 'religion-can-be-enjoyable' style of worship. In the 1960s he formed his own alternative congregation and worshippers flocked first to his mission in Byker, Newcastle. Later, in 1980, Frank raised money to buy a redundant 1,000-seater Methodist church in North Shields, which he ran successfully for many years. Here he employed his psychology degree to incentivise giving, utilising large, clear plastic confectionary jars in place of collection plates, placing a few 'encouraging' £5 notes in the bottom.

Traditionally churchwardens managed the role of treasurer, gathering small donations and collecting money on Sundays which would be stored safely for later distribution to the poor and needy of the parish. With the introduction of PCCs, the churchwardens were relieved of their role as parish treasurer. The PCC are required to elect a treasurer annually however if one cannot be elected, then the role falls to the churchwardens until such time as the post can be filled. Today the churchwardens are still responsible for gathering and counting the collection (offertory), ably assisted by the sidesmen, who are responsible to them.

The offertory, that oft-embarrassing part of the service, is undergoing a comprehensive review that may drag it kicking and screaming into the 21st century. Ingenious ways have been devised to avoid the guilt of the 'Sunday morning stickup'. Beware, churchwardens. The centuries-old ritual of passing round the collection plate is going digital, with plans from the Church of England to use the 'tap and go' contactless payment system for donations. The church trial will test the practicalities of various 'platforms', from offering the card reader as an option alongside the collection plate, to installing a terminal at the back of the church as a 'retiring collection point'. To save time, parishioners are likely to be asked to choose one of three common donations or select 'other' and tap in an amount of their choice. The Church hopes to boost collections from those attending weddings, christenings or those who attend services so seldom that they forget to bring any cash for that moment the collection plate suddenly arrives.

Alternatively, some churches are considering cryptocurrencies (a peer-to-peer electronic cash system). Avoiding the inevitable psycho-babble, they advise that one preferred option is the 'Christ Coin', which can be used to financially reward people who read the Bible and interact with the community on its 'Life Change Platform'. An alternative is the 'Jesus Coin', which 'provides global access to Jesus that's safer and faster than ever before'.

The retiring collection was supposed to be voluntary

Vacancies are an inevitable part of parish life. They are a time to reflect on the future but they may also involve anxiety and difficulties. Vacancies may be triggered by retirement, promotion, resignation, the vicar refocussing their ministry, or sadly the death of an incumbent. The vicar leaving may come as a surprise, or it may have been expected for some time. For some members of the congregation, it will be a time of great sadness. For others, it may even be a relief! The first rule of thumb is not to panic – help is at hand. Take a deep breath and let it all sink in before taking actions that may be regretted later. The parish management of the interregnum is down to the churchwardens and it is a test of their capabilities to draw together the PCC to plan for the short-term and put in place contingency plans for the long haul. Vacancies are risky times and statistics published by the London diocese indicate that few parishes emerge from a vacancy period, certainly not long ones, without some numerical losses. In most cases, there will be time to work closely with the incumbent and plan for their leaving, however this is not always true.

Churchwardens must be constantly aware of changing circumstances within and outside of their parish, and the PCC must be open to discussion on sensitive issues and have policies and processes in place to deal with any outcome. In recent times, there have been situations that have caused distress within a parish, resulting in trauma for its congregation. Two examples would be the decision to institute personal ordinariates for Anglicans who join the Catholic Church, and the recent issues surrounding homosexual clergy. The ordinariates were announced in October 2009. This complex and contentious process, mired in controversy, allows Anglicans closer to the Catholic faith to be part of the Catholic tradition, whilst maintaining some of their Anglican practices. There are examples of Anglican ministers upping sticks virtually overnight, taking some of their flock with them and leaving behind distress and heartache . Since the 1990 s, the Anglican Communion has struggled with such matters . Whatever your viewpoint , they have impacted on some communities , challenging Christian values and biblical interpretation.

I was reminded of a story I read about a vicar who was leaving a parish. He preached a wonderful last sermon and as people were shaking his hand at the door, an old chap said to the vicar, 'We'll miss you; the next vicar won't be as good as you!' The vicar was flattered and humbly said, 'Oh, no, I'm sure that won't be true.' 'Oh, it will be,' said the man. 'You see, I've been a member of this church for forty years and have seen five vicars come and go...and each one was worse than the last!'

Chapter 27

ENTREPRENEURS AND IMPRESARIOS

Nowadays, churches are being actively encouraged to devise ways to increase the use of church spaces for the purposes of community outreach and enterprise. As I discussed in an earlier chapter, our warden predecessors were encouraged in a similar way (but not for the same reasons) to build church houses, which may be considered as the medieval equivalent of the modern church hall. The purpose of this development was to remove the sometimes less-savoury activities away from the church building itself and to create a space for the many festivals and 'church ales', which raised funds for many an English parish church (until the rise of Puritanism).

These, often substantial, buildings of two storeys served the parishes well and the entrepreneurial skills of the churchwardens ensured that the use of the church house was maximised. During the 16th and 17th centuries, groups of theatrical players toured the country, performing at such venues. These events must have been something to see. One such 'royal event' at Christ Church Oxford, witnessed by the Queen, was described as a *Spectacular Apparitisima* (sumptuous spectacle) complete with drama, jousting and carnival parades. During the early 17th century, a warrant was issued authorising William Shakespeare and his companions to perform plays throughout the realm under royal patronage. 'The King's Men', as they were known, was the acting company to which William Shakespeare belonged for most of his career. During the mid-17th century these tours increased, after theatres recovered from their closure during the Great Plague of London in 1603. However, in 1642, The Puritan Parliament issued an ordinance suppressing all stage plays, which resulted in clandestine performances taking place.

The *Passion Play* has been performed in Oberammergau since 1633, so you would have thought that 'educated people' would be aware of its origins and message by now. Not so, however, in Oxford, the great seat of learning, where (in 2014) an over enthusiastic council official banned a performance of the Good Friday *Passion Play* at Cowley Road Methodist Church, because he thought it was a live sex show that might have caused offence! The official later apologised, explaining that 'the licensing officers did not recognise that a *Passion Play* on Good Friday was a religious event'.[75] He was obviously too passionate about his job and oblivious to the passion of others.

Punch - (or *The London Charivari*) was a British weekly satirical magazine, mixed with a certain degree of irreverence. *Punch* adopted and promoted the use of cartoons in its humorous illustrations. Volume 6, published in 1844, presented a pantomime called Harlequin Chuchwarden (or the Wizard of Walbrook). Set in the select vestry of St Stephen's Church, it focused on a set of missing accounts, which later magically appeared with a sprite holding the illusive balance sheet!

Chapter 28

TEMPUS NEMINEM MANET

Unusually, many Maltese churches have two clocks, showing different times. Local folklore tells us that the one on the right shows the correct time for religious locals, whilst the one on the left shows the wrong time to distract Satan from disturbing the mass. Before the middle of the 20th century, most people did not have watches, and prior to the 18th century, even home clocks were rare. The first clocks were the striking clocks that called those in the surrounding community to work or to prayer. They were placed in church towers so that the bells would be audible from a long distance. Only later did it occur to add a dial on the outside of the tower to allow the townspeople to read the time whenever they wanted.

Britain has had a rich history of timekeeping since King Charles II founded the Royal Society and the Royal Observatory at Greenwich in 1660. 'The UK is the epicentre of global timekeeping but clocks are also about so much more. Clocks are part of the community; part of being British'.[76] The ringing of church bells has in recent years become a contentious issue, prompting many complaints to local council noise abatement teams, particularly regarding the 24/7 chiming of church clocks. After living in the busy suburbs for many years, I never tire of the sounds (and sometimes smells) of the rural life I now enjoy, sitting in the garden on a warm summer's evening (wishful thinking). What is more pleasing to the ear than hearing the melodic chimes of the parish church clock as it strikes the Westminster quarters across the village, complementing the lambs plaintively bleating in the fields and the birds settling to rest? (Sorry, I'm getting carried away). But who ensures that the church clock keeps vigil on the village, advising us of the hours (and quarters) and prompting us to church each Sunday? Let us spare a thought for the trusty clock-winder struggling up the narrow spiral staircase of the church tower, perhaps twice a week to give us timely pleasure. Historic churchwardens' accounts show that they often paid someone to wind the church clock, but on occasions that duty has fallen to the churchwardens themselves. This is the case at St Michael's in Helston, Cornwall, whose clock has been wound manually since it was installed in 1793. Three times a week, a warden perches eight feet up a ladder and stretches to wind the mechanism. Recently, however, the church has been advised by the local council and the Diocesan Guild of Ringers to cease this procedure on health and safety grounds. So, like many other churches, they are now fundraising to facilitate the purchase of an automated clock winding machine.

In Clapham, North Yorkshire, the parish church clock had been carefully tended by the local GP for more than 50 years. He climbed the tower twice a week to wind it. John Farrer died, aged 92, at 8:13 a.m.

on New Year's Day 2014, and eerily the hands of the Victorian timepiece froze at that same moment. The vicar of St James's said 'It was a remarkable coincidence. The event recalls the parlour song "My Grandfather's Clock", which, as the refrain says, "it stopped short, never to go again, when the old man died"'.[77] *Tempus Fugit.*

Chapter 29

THE FUTURE

Traditionally, churchwardens were men of substance, able to commit time as well as talents and money to churchmanship. With the pace of modern society, it is becoming more and more difficult to fill the parish administrative roles.

"Thanks for your concern, Mrs Watkins but the 'suspicious youths hanging around the church' are actually our new churchwardens."

Whilst there are many younger people who feel able to offer service to their church, the practicalities of the modern world hold them back from volunteering. Faced with a dearth of people able to fill positions of lay leadership in church, PCCs are having to become innovative in their approach to fulfilling traditional roles. St Mary the Virgin, Davyhulme, in the diocese of Manchester, has launched a 'wardenshare' programme, making the position of churchwarden more flexible and part-time, in an effort to encourage younger working people, or those who have children, to fill the role. To enable the programme to work, older and more experienced former churchwardens are offering mentoring advice and cover for some weekday responsibilities. Through this approach of shared experience, a cross-generational pool of people is being created, better able to serve in lay leadership positions.[78]

The Churchwarden's Lament

Chosen by parishioners with complete equanimity,
Churchwardens serve the them with discrete sensitivity.

Ready at first to commit, I'm now doubting that I'm fit.
Will I do it? Can I do it? or shall I just eschew it?

The Canons are loaded but have vague job description,
there are many spare lines without prescription.

Part of our role is encouraging Susans and Trevors,
by employing our stave with skills and endeavours.

Over the years the role has matured, in line with society,
though we're no longer involved with parishioner propriety

Custodians of church property and bearing the onus
we have great responsibility but none of the bonus

Organising the seating requires great democracy, a pain,
however achieving worshipper satisfaction is our aim.

Despite many tasks being shrouded in jargon and faculty,
wardens approach them with feigned alacrity.

Terriers, Log Books and Inventories all need attention
before the Archdeacon makes his inspection.

Six years continuous service is now the restriction,
not a day longer to avoid addiction.

So, like compadres of old let us gather and make a brew,
to celebrate proud service with a church ale or two.

Eric Sanderson

The Churchwardens Measure 2001 reinforces the importance of providing current and future churchwardens, as well as other lay people holding office in the parish, with training and information about training. This should enable them to discharge their duties satisfactorily and also encourage those who are thinking of serving.

There are many similarities between the roles of the churchwarden and the verger. Like the churchwarden, the role of verger is an ancient one. Some might say it is older than Christianity itself, with its origins going back to the temple servants of the Old Testament. These were Jewish temple gatekeepers, in charge of guarding the house of the Lord and the treasures therein.

There are no 'standard' job descriptions for either the role of churchwarden or verger. However, the churchwardens' main duties are clearly stated in the Canons of the Church of England E1 paragraphs 4 and 5, and the wardens are always nominated by the parishioners and installed by their diocesan bishop. Over the centuries, the verger's role has morphed into the sometimes complex one it is today. It ranges from cleaning and hospitality, to health and safety and security, to sacristan and everything in between. They are, however, appointed by either the PCC, or in the case of cathedrals, by the dean and chapter, performing roles unique to their location.

Norwegian researchers have found that attending church not only lowers blood pressure, but it continues to do so with more frequent attendance. This may be true of church services, but in my experience, churchwardens often feel stressed, overburdened by the minutia of parochial problems with no network to support them. They perhaps rely on the support of peers who have suffered similar experiences. Having served as churchwarden and having had regular contact over the years with others, I have become disillusioned with the lack of a support structure for the churchwarden. Whilst initial training is provided by the diocese, churchwardens often return to their parishes reliant on the mentorship of peers.

The Church of England Guild of Vergers was founded in 1932 and is endorsed by the Archbishops of Canterbury and York. Its purpose is to support and encourage vergers through a diploma training course established to cover the work and ministry of the verger. This bursary-funded correspondence course was started on the recommendation of the General Synod, and on completion the 'students' receive the post-nominal letters 'DIP.G.V.' With a possible 25,000 churchwardens in the UK, the need for an improved network is long overdue. The potential for spreading experiences is a vast and untapped resource of immeasurable knowledge.

Chapter 30

HAS CHURCH GONE BARKING MAD?

Paws for thought? - No sooner than churchwardens had paid off the dog whipper, someone had the idea to let dogs back into church. Dr Laura Hobgood-Oster is Professor of Religion and Environmental Studies at Southwestern University in Georgetown, Texas. For many years, she has studied the intricate relationship between humans and other animals and she has discovered that animals have always been central to many of the world's major religions. She maintains that the history of Christianity is full of animal blessings and animal burials. Many holy people (especially saints) are pictured with animals and have had caring and loving relationships with them. There was a tradition full of animals – we just started to lose sight of that three or four hundred years ago.

Given experiences of the past, churches (and particularly churchwardens) are circumspect in the matter of allowing God's creatures into church, whether from a practical, hygiene or health and safety perspective. Churchwardens particularly may be concerned that their skills are deficient, requiring additional training in veterinary science and animal psychology to deal with potential 'behavioural incidents'.

Nowadays we hear of churches becoming 'all inclusive' but this generally refers to members of the human race and assistance dogs. The festival day for St Francis of Assisi, the patron saint of animals, has become the time when many Christian faiths now hold special church services to bless pets. There are an increasing number of churches adopting a 'pets-welcome policy' though I suspect that it will be a long while before there is a canon law to regulate such activity!

The historic Christ Church on New York's Upper East Side New York annually takes the bull by the horns (not literally I hope) and hosts their annual, hour long, Blessing of the Animals Service. In 2018 the church was packed as around 700 animals and their owners listened to a sermon based on the narrative of Noah's Ark. There was a carnival of animals as anything with fur, fins, feathers and fluff took part and processed down the aisle to be sprinkled with water and receive a blessing.

Christening (Carlisle, 2010) - Most pet owners have fondness for their animals but few go that step further to publicly demonstrate their feelings. A Cumbrian pet owner loved his dog so much that he didn't pause for thought when he decided that he would like the dog christened, making a public display of his affection to friends and family.

A venue was arranged and a local dog owning vicar agreed to a blessing in church, to be followed by a laying on of hands in a nearby hotel. No expense was spared on the event. A pre-event beauty make-over, a silk shawl and chauffeured transport to the church where the bells were ringing. The ceremony which included godmothers and godfathers was followed by a lavish meal with 75 guests and toasts with Champagne. [79]

Pet ministry - When the Rev. Tom Eggebeen took over as interim pastor at Covenant Presbyterian Church, he knew it needed a jump start. Most of his worshippers, though devoted, were in their 60s. Attendance had bottomed out and the once-vibrant church was fading fast. Eggebeen came up with an oblique idea: he would turn God's house into a doghouse by offering a 30-minute service complete with individual doggie beds, canine prayers and an offering of dog treats. He hoped to attract new worshippers who were as crazy about God as they were about their four-legged friends. The weekly dog service at Covenant is part of a growing trend among churches across the United States to address the spirituality of pets and the deeply-felt bonds that owners form with their animals. One church in Boston is called Woof 'n Worship!

In Britain, the ethos of the Anglican Society for the Welfare of Animals (ASWA) is Biblical teaching, that God has given us 'dominion' not 'domination' over animals (Genesis 1:26); 'loving care' not 'ruthless exploitation', a non-negotiable part of Christian discipleship. ASWA encourages churches to hold animal friendly services and they organise an annual service on Animal Welfare Sunday, the nearest to St. Francistide (4th of October) promoting the welfare of all of God's creatures. Annually, they gather with other like-minded groups at the Animals in War Memorial, in Park Lane, London to lay wreaths at a service dedicated to the recognition of animals in war and conflict.

Chapter 31

In praise of Churchwardens

The role of a churchwarden is vital to the life and health of a parish. This, the highest lay position in the Anglican church vests in them the valuable artefacts and other movables in the church along with the custodianship and maintenance of buildings. This unfortunately appears to indicate that the role has all the disadvantages of ownership without any of the advantages!

Leadership by example encourages others to offer their gifts and talents in the service of God's church. The wise care of the finances, buildings and people of the parish ensure that ministry may be accomplished, both today and in the days to come.

Churchwardens duties are rarely written down, Canon Law cursorily advising "they shall discharge such duties as are by law and custom assigned to them." It goes on to say that Churchwardens "shall use their best endeavours by example and precept to encourage the parishioners in the practice of true religion and to promote unity and peace among them." Reinforcing the gravity of the position.

Remember - The position of Church Warden is not a life sentence: church rules limit the time of continuous service to six consecutive years *(unless the Annual Meeting passes a resolution to set aside this rule).* A statutory break of two years ensures time for refreshment and reflection.

I would also recommend to you 'The Old Churchwarden: Mr Christopher Hey' by W.B. Russell Caley: a eulogy to Christopher Hey, the churchwarden of St Mary's in Watton, Thetford. With great eloquence, it expresses how grateful we should all be for churchwardens.[80]

Rejuvenation

Bertie, one of the Wardens up at the church, has a special doctor's appointment tomorrow morning.

I believe, from what they say in the village, that he must be nearing eighty. Certainly he's an old boy of Little Tremlett School, which closed its doors back in the forties. Yet he barely looks a day over fifty. They reckon that his remarkable youth is down to his receiving a dose of special "reviving" hormones periodically, which village rumour connects to concepts such as "monkey glands" and "something a civet would rather not live without".

Anyway, tomorrow he's off to the doctor's for his latest dose. Apparently each booster lasts five years. The women at the church refer to it as his "Quinquennial injection".

"From Writes of the Church by Gary Alderson (BRF, 2017)

BIBLIOGRAPHY

[1] Charles Grevile Prideaux, *A Practical Guide to the Duties of Churchwardens in the Execution of their Office* (London: Shaw and Sons, 1845), iii.

[2] John Stidolph, *The Churchwarden's Yearbook 2016* (Churchwarden Publications Limited, 2015).

[3] Katherine L. French, *The People of the Parish: Community Life in a Late Medieval English Diocese* (Pennsylvania: University of Pennsylvania Press, 2012), 45.

[4] *Katherine L. French, The People of the Parish:* Community Life in a Late Medieval English Diocese, 44-68.

[5] Charles Grevile Prideaux, *A Practical Guide to the Duties of Churchwardens*, 10.

[6] *Life in the 11th Century,* The Domesday Book Online, http://www.domesdaybook.co.uk/life.html.

[7] C N Trueman, *The Dissolution of the Monasteries,* History Learning Site, 16 March 2015, https://www.historylearningsite.co.uk/tudor-england/the-dissolution-of-the-monasteries/.-

[8] Heather Sharnette (M.Phil) - *Elizabeth R* (self published) 1998-2019) - htpswww.elizabethi.org

[9] Philip Edgcumbe Hughes, *Preaching, Homilies & Prophesyings in 16th Century England* - Churchman 89/1 1975

[10] *The Dissolution of the Monasteries*, Request, https://request.org.uk/people/history/the-dissolution-of-the-monastries/

[11] C J Sansom, *Prince of Darkness: The truth about Thomas Cromwell*, The Daily Mail, 9 October 2009, https://www.dailymail.co.uk/news/article-1219158/Prince-Darkness-The-truth-Thomas-Cromwell.html.

[12] William Edward Tate, The Parish Chest: *A Study of the Records of Parochial Administration in England* (Cambridge: Cambridge University Press, 1969).

[13] Giles Jacob, *The Compleat Parish Officer* (1734), reprinted by the Wiltshire Family History Society, 1996; **also**, Henry Clavering, *The New and Complete Parish Officer* (London: Gale, Curtis and Fenner, 1812).

[14] Marjie Bloy, *The Sturges-Bourne Act* (1819), The Victorian Web, 7 November 2002, http://www.victorianweb.org/history/poorlaw/sturgesb.html.

[15] Sarah Richardson, *The Political Worlds of Women: Gender and Politics in Nineteenth Century Britain* (Abingdon: Routledge, 2013) - 188

[16] Charlotte Carmichael Stopes, *British Freewomen: A Historical Privilege* (Cambridge: Cambridge University Press, 2010) 157.

[17] Tim Stretton, *Women, Property and Law, in A Companion to Early Modern Women's Writing*, ed. Anita Pacheco (Oxford: Blackwell Publishing, 2002) 42.

[18] Sarah Richardson, *Petticoat Politicians - Women and the Politics of the Parish in England.* The Historian (August 2013)

[19] N.S.Gill - *Hierarchy of Roman Offices in The Cursus Honorum* - http://www.thoughtco.com/cursus-honorum-roman-offices-120107

[20] Humphrey Prideaux, *Directions to Church-Wardens,* https://biblehub.com/library/prideaux/directions_to_church-wardens/directions_to_church-wardens_&c.htm.

[21] David Phillips, *Freehold and the Church of England PLC, Cross†Way, Issue 96, Spring 2005*, http://archive.churchsociety.org/crossway/documents/Cway_096_Freehold.pdf.

[22] Church Times - *Christchurch Spitalfields* (various authors) - Articles between November 2012 and March 2017. **Also**:- Chancellor June Rodgers, sitting as a Deputy Chancellor of the Diocese of London in the Consistory Court of the diocese of London - Transcript (497 pages) entitled '*In the matter of a building in the churchyard of Christ Church Spitalfields and In the matter of an application for a restoration order and a petition for a confirmatory faculty.*' **Also** - https://www.wilberforce.co.uk/christ-church-spitalfields-the-battle-of-the-churchyard/

[23] Shiranikha Herbert (Church Times legal Correspondent) *Wardens incur legal costs after unauthorised sale* (21.07.2011)

[24] Shiranikha Herbert, *Lottery Plaque judged too tasteless for church porch.* (17.02.2017)

[25] *Certain Sermons or Homilies Appointed to be Read in Churches* (Oxford: Oxford University Press, 1840) 544.

[26] Law and Order at St.Neots. *Whipping Post* - bernardoconnor.org.uk/Publications/Stneots/Laworder.htm

[27] Fuller v Lane (1825) 162 English Reports 348.

[28] Adrian Tinniswood, *His Invention So Fertile, Alife of Christopher Wren* - Pimlico Press (2002) page 376

[29] Jennifer Fulwiler, *The Socially Awkward Person's Guide to the Sign of Peace,* National Catholic Register, 3 June 2011, http://www.ncregister.com/blog/jennifer-fulwiler/the-socially-awkward-persons-guide-to-the-sign-of-peace.

[30] Liza Picard - British Library 2016 - *Church and punishment in Elizabethan England*

[31] Humphrey Prideaux, *Directions to Church-Wardens: for the Faithful Discharge of their Office*, (London: F. Collins, 1713) 3-4.

[32] *Cock fighting in Knotting Church*, Bedfordshire Archives and Record Services, http://bedsarchives.bedford.gov.uk/CommunityArchives/Knotting/Cock-Fighting-in-Knotting-Chur9h.aspx.

[33] The Berkshire Record Office Newsletter, Issue 36, Summer 2006. http://www.berkshirerecordoffice.org.uk/berkshire-echo/2006-archive/berkshire-echo-36/.

[34] St. Martin's Church Stoney Middleton, *Some links with the past & A working Village* - Millenium Awards (2002)

[35] A.M Bagley, *A Guide to the Parish Church of SS Peter and Paul, Hathern,* 2005. http://ww.hathernhistory.co.uk/images/hathern/scans/guide_to_church.pdf.

[36] Miss Lucy F March Phillips. *My Life, and What Shall I Do With It?* (1862) Records of the ministry of the Rev E.T. March-Phillips.

[37] Hathern History - *The trials and tribulations of E.Smythies* - http://www.hathernhistory.co.uk/index.php/home/featured-articles

[38] Brett Birks - *The Knocknobbler* - bbc March 2007

[39] *When I grow up I want to be a...dog whipper.* Window through Time, 29 May 2013, https://windowthroughtime.wordpress.com/tag/dog-whipper/.

[40] Thomas Tusser *(1524 – 1580)* http://www.archive.org/stream/fivehundredpoint08tussuoft/fivehundredpoint08tussuoft_djvu.txt -

[41] *Cathedral Constables* - http://www.cathedralconstables.co.uk/

[42] *Raising a Voluntary Church Rate* - http://hampsteadparishchurch.org.uk/data/vol_rate.php.

[43] *Poor Law Unions' Gazette,* The British Newspaper Archive, https://www.britishnewspaperarchive.co.uk/titles/poor-law-unions-gazette.

[44] Ancient History Encyclopaedia - *The Hymn to Ninkasi, Goddess of Beer* - https://www.ancient.eu/article/222/the-hymn-to-ninkasi-goddess-of-beer/

[45] *Every loaf of bread is a tragic story of grains that could've become beer, but didn't.* -Walter Thornburg (identity

[46] Clerical Whispers - *Beer for a fast in Lent* 01/03/2017/47

[47] Beat Kümin, *The secular legacy of the late medieval English Parish Church.* Harlaxton Symposium, Harlaxton College, 23-26 Jul 2002 pp. 95-111.

[48] Ben Johnson, *The London Beer Flood of 1814.* Historic UK, www.historic-uk.com/HistoryUK/HistoryofBritain/The-London-Beer-Flood-of-1814/.

[49] William Prynne *Histriomastix* - British Civil Wars, Commonwealth and Protectorate http://bcw-project.org/biography/william-prynne

[50] Sean Coughlan (BBC News Correspondent), *Elizabethan child actors kidnapped and whipped.* 18/6/2013

[51] Donald L. Roberts, *John Wycliffe and the Dawn of the Reformation,* Christian History, Issue 3, 1983, https://christianhistoryinstitute.org/magazine/article/john-wycliffe-and-the-dawn-of-the-reformation.

[52] *Joseph, Exchequer, of the Jews.* Jewish Historical Society. https://jhse.org.

[53] *Recusant Rolls* (Catholics) -www.genguide.c.uk/source/recusant-rolls-catholics

[54] David Crowther, *John Colet and the Convocation of 1512,* https://thehistoryofengland.co.uk/resource/john-colet-and-the-convocation-of-1512/.

[55] Margaret Spufford, *The World of Rural Dissenters,* 1520-1725 (Cambridge: Cambridge University Press, 1995) 177.

[56] *Episcopal Visitation Returns, 1744 and 1779.* Friends of Devon's Archives, www.foda.org.uk/visitations/intro/1744queries.htm.

[57] W. J. Sheils, *Bishops and their dioceses: reform of visitation in the Anglican church c.1680–c.1760.* CCEd Online Journal 1, 2007. http://ww.theclergydatabase.org.uk/cce_a1/

[58] Church Times - https://www.churchtimes.co.uk/articles/2016/7-october/news/uk/cathedrals-too-uppity-dean-fears

[59] Simon Newman, *Witches and Witchcraft in the Middle Ages.* The Finer Times. www.thefinertimes.com/Middle-Ages/witches-and-witchcraft-in-the-middle-ages.html.

[60] Professor Douglas O. Linder. *A brief history of witchcraft persecutions before Salem.*

[61] *Her Majesty the Queen approves recommendations for Westminster Abbey* Monday, 9th February 2004 - www.westminster-abbey.org/abbey-news/her-majesty-the-queen-approves-recommendations-for-westminster-abbey

[62] Jesse Addams, *Reports of Cases Argued and Determined in the Ecclesiastical Courts* (London: S. Sweet, 1825) 200.

[63] William Calverley Curteis, *Reports of Cases Argued and Determined in the Ecclesiastical Courts* (London: Saunders and Benning, 1840) 452-3. - 192 –

[64] *How to address the Clergy, Crockford's Clerical Dictionary*, www.crockford.org.uk/faq/how-to-address-the-clergy.

[65] *Being a Churchwarden*, Diocese of Chichester, No.5, http://www.chichester.anglican.org/media/documents/document/2015/07/Being_a_Churchwarden.pdf.

[66] Charles Grevile Prideaux, *A Practical Guide to the Duties of Churchwardens*, 250.

[67] Henry William Cripps, *A Practical Treatise on the Laws Relating to the Church and the Clergy* (London: S. Sweet, 1845)

[68] John Bingham (The Telegraph Religious Affairs Editor) 25.10.2015) *Comments made by Rt. Reverend Peter Broadbent.*

[69] Andrew Brown, *Bishops babes:* Archbishop of Canterbury Justin Welby and women priests celebrating the 20th anniversary of female ordination. The Oldie, September 2014, https://www.theoldie.co.uk/article/vestments-into-frocks.

[70] The Daily Telegraph, October 2012, *More teal vicar? Colourful clergy show off new robes on Catwalk.* https://www.telegraph.co.uk/news/religion/9593812/More-teal-vicar-Colourful-clergy-show-off-new-robes-on-catwalk.html.

[71] https://www.collaredclergywear.co.uk/.

***Eastlondonhistory.com - 16 June 2011, http://eastlondonhistory.com/2011/06/16/joseph-merceron-of-brick-lane/.

[73] Linda Ali, *Christianity and the Transatlantic Slave Trade,* www.shapworkingparty.org.uk/journals articles_0607/Ali.rtf.

Also see:- *SlaveTrade Ethics* - www.bbc.co.uk/ethics/slavery/ethics/philosophers. and James Walvin, *The Slave Trade and the Churches* (York University) - Quaker Studies 12/2 (2008) 189-195

[74] The Times, January 2012, *Churchwardens quit in row with rector.* https://www.thetimes.co.uk/article/churchwardens-quit-in-row-with-rector-0hdbzr829gd.

[75] The Huffington Post, April 2014, *Labour Council Bans Passion Of The Christ Play Mistaken For Live Sex Show.* https://www.huffingtonpost.co.uk/2014/04/17/labour-council-passion-of_n_5166599.html.

~~Also Ama~~tonia Molloy, The Independent, *Oxford City Council apologises after Passion Play it mistook for live sex show is cancelled.* Also - www.independent.uk/news. 18/4/2014

[76] Denis Winterman, *Time stands still.* BBC News Magazine, August 2007.

[77] Paul Wilkinson, *Clock stopped when the old man died,* Church Times, February 2014, https://www.churchtimes.co.uk/articles/2014/14-february/news/uk/clock-stopped-when-the-old-man-died.

[78] Tim Wyatt (Church Times 2/2/2018). *Flexible scheme to attract younger churchwardens.*

[79] Robert Mendick, *Dog gets elaborate church blessing,* The Daily Telegraph, November 2010, https://www.telegraph.co.uk/news/newstopics/howaboutthat/8148567/Dog-gets-elaborate-church-blessing.html.

[80] W.B. Russell Caley, *The Old Churchwarden: Mr Christopher Hey.* https://biblicalstudies.org.uk/pdf/churchman/012-07_359.pdf.

Additional Reading

The English Clergy Association, *Churchwardens in a Nutshell*, http://www.clergyassoc.co.uk/content/churchwardens.htm.

J. P. Gent, *A New Guide for Constables, Headboroughs, Tythingmen, Church-wardens, Overseers and Collectors for the Poor, Surveyors for Amending the Highways and Bridges* (London: 1692).

John Wigger, PTL: *The Rise and Fall of Jim and Tammy Faye Bakker's Evangelical Empire* (Oxford University Press 2017)

George Henry, *Churchwardens' Manual - their duties, powers, rights, and privileges* (London: Simpkin and Co. 1897).

John Paul, *The Parish Officer's Complete Guide. Containing the Duty of the Churchwarden, Overseer, Constable, and Surveyor of the Highways* (London: W. Strahan and M. Woodhall, 1776).

Peter M Smith, *An Introduction to the Nature of the Office*, Churchman 114/2, 2000, http://archive.churchsociety.org/churchman/documents/cman_114_2_smith.pdf.

Thomas Edlyne Tomlins, *The Law-dictionary: Explaining the Rise, Progress and Present State of the British Law*: Vol. II (London: Payne, 1820).

Derek Fraser, *Urban Politics in Victorian England*, Macmillan Press Ltd.

CARTOON CREDITS

By kind permission of the following:

Reverend Ron Wood – Cartoonist to the Church Times (St. Gargoyle's).

Noel Ford – Editorial Cartoonist on the Church Times.

Dennis Fletcher – An American, Christian (lay pastor), freelance writer and cartoonist.

David Parkins – British Freelance illustrator (particularly comics) and cartoonist now working in Canada.

IMAGES - COPYRIGHT INFORMATION

Finger Pillory at St. Helen's Church
Ashby-de-la-Zouch – Jimfbleak, own work.
https://commons.wikimedia.org/w/index.php?curid=36806718

White Rubik Cube (Rubik 3D) – Openclipart.org

Sign Post – By courtesy of: Stuart Miles / FreeDigitalPhotos.net

clipartelibrary.com

EPILOGUE

The aim of this book was to reassure churchwardens that their life is easier than that of their predecessors . It did not intend to be a complete history of the churchwarden . The Vestry system within which the churchwardens operated was at times politically intense . By the early 17th century , parish meetings were so well organised that they acquired responsibility for all manner of local government activity and became 'pocket parliaments '. The churchwarden was the business manager of the parish and responsible for setting and gathering local taxes . At the height of their powers , in 1834, the vestries spent around of one-fifth of the budget of the national government itself . The government was keen to get hold of this money and churchwardens became mired in the manoeuvring between the political parties of the time as the government fought to wrestle financial control from the vestries . This activity employed all manner of devious 'tools' from electioneering to bribery . It all came to a head with the passing of the Vestries Act in 1850 - legislation designed to regulate the local government of parishes . Thereafter the election of churchwardens became solely a matter of ecclesiastical concern and government interference ceased . The churchwarden 's role had gone full-circle , from purely ecclesiastical beginnings through turbulent political times returning to the principles of its origins – looking after the church , its property and its people.